KJV BIBLE CRYPTOGRAMS

The Psalms

I0616450

GOOD AND RIGHT PUBLISHING

Reviews are very important to small businesses like ours. Please take a moment to leave us feedback, wherever you purchased this book. Thank you!

Instructions

Use your deciphering skills to decode these scriptures from the King James Bible.

Each letter is substituted for another letter and you must figure out the pattern to reveal the Bible verses. You will be given one to three letters in each puzzle. The code is different for each passage, even if there is more than one cryptogram on the same page.

All of the selections in this book are taken from Psalms and a few contain more than one verse. The references are left off the puzzle pages but are included in the solutions.

Please enjoy!

1

_I__ __ ____ _R__ _R_____: __R __I_
ABTQ PZ GQKS OIVN EIVPRKQ: OVI TJBM

I_ ___ ____ __ ___.
BZ EGQ GQKS VO NJM.

2

____ ____ __MM_____ __ __ ____ __Y
XQMK QWPX OMUUWZCVC KP XM NVVD XQS

_____ _____Y.
DGVOVDXP CLJLIVZXJS.

3

_____ _____D ___ _____ ___,
YKDSDUNSD TKNVIC BKD KDPBKDO TPZ,

_____ __ ___ _____ G_D?
YKDSD MT ONY BKDMS HNC?

4

___ L___ __O____ ___ __O_____ O_ ___,
AIK UJBN FGJYKAI AIK AIJOZIAQ JS LXG,

____ ____ ___ _____.
AIXA AIKC XBK MXGWAC.

5

___ ___D ____ ____ ___V__ ___ _____
DUI XVLW DUHD GHWI UIHKIZ HZW IHLDU

_____ ____ ___ __ ____.
MXIBB DUII VPD VY ROVZ.

6

```
_ ____ ___ ___D, H__ _____ __  _H_
L QLVH LCV QLVH, JLA BZGBQQBUE RT EJI

____ __ ___ _H_ ____H!
UYPB RU YQQ EJB BYVEJ!
```

7

```
___ __ _U_ ___U__ ___ _____, _
RBO EV BTH HPSTRP JGO VKHPGRKU, J

____ _____ __L_ __ ___U_L_.
WPHN QHPVPGK UPDQ EG KHBTXDP.
```

8

```
__ ___I___I__ __ _I_ _____ __ _____:
UO ULCXRTRXPA PI BXU WBTEE HL WQLLR:

_ _I__ __ ____ I_ ___ ___D.
X QXEE HL FETC XA RBL EPZC.
```

9

```
_____, _ L___, _N__ ___ ____; ____,
WXVED, N KNXU, VBYN YIO XDEY; YINP,

_N_ ___ ___ __ ___ ____N___.
WBU YID WXQ NJ YIO EYXDBLYI.
```

10

```
__ _S _____ __ ___S_ __ ___ ____
NA NM ZCAACS AP ASJMA NV AEC OPSF

____ __ ___ ___F_____ __ ___.
AEXV AP DJA BPVGNFCVBC NV RXV.
```

11

```
___T _____ _ _____ __T_ T__ __R_
QKEU XKERR Y DSCZSD GCUM UKS RMDZ

___ ___ ___ _____T_ T_____ __?
BMD ERR KYX VSCSBYUX UMQEDZ LS?
```

12

```
T__ ____ __ __ __ ____; _ ____ ___
SFV XZDQ HP ZB RN PHQV; H OHXX BZS

__R: ____ ___ ___ __ ____ __?
WVKD: OFKS GKB RKB QZ TBSZ RV?
```

13

```
__ ____, ____, _____ ____
EM KSWP, NWXQ, VSWPNQCVK IDXF

I_I__I_I__, _ ____, W__ _____ _____?
EGEBPEKECV, W NWXQ, OSW VSDNN VKDGQ?
```

14

```
___ _____ _____ ____ ___ ___K ___ __
RVX ZKUML AKFML PXMK LTE SKFJ VXH MK

___ _____ ____ ___ _V_____.
LTE QVIKPF PXMTQ MLU UGUXTXZ.
```

15

```
___ ___D __ _____: __ ____ ___
GOL NITB KP TKFOGLIVP: OL OQGO YVG

____D__ ___ ___D_ __ ___ _____D.
QPVDBLT GOL YITBP IR GOL EKYJLB.
```

16

`__ ____S ___ ____ T_____ __ST___; ___`
QG VTLLX CZL SLCV RBZEYUB HCXRPTU; CTJ

`__ ___S_ _____T_ __ __T__SS.`
QG HILXB HCPILRB EH HCRTLXX.

17

`____ F__ ___ _____ _F J_____:`
JONK GAO VWH JHNBH AG PHOZFNCHS:

`____ _____ _____ ____ ____ ____.`
VWHK FWNCC JOAFJHO VWNV CAIH VWHH.

18

`___ ____ _____T_ T__ _____: I`
OUN JDAP LANTNAHNOU OUN TEWLJN: E

`___ _____T ___, ___ __ _____ __.`
GYT ZADCVUO JDG, YMP UN UNJLNP WN.

19

`___ ____ _____ ___ ___ __R_, _____`
ZFG YGXY SAXUWG RIZ ZFG KIAY, RGUZFGA

`__Y ____ __ ____ ____ _____.`
XRJ ZFXZ HI YINR URZI WUKGRBG.

20

`I _I__ _I__ ____ ___ ____, _____`
L ILMM WLKX FKRT RAH MTPV, OHUZFWH

`__ ____ _____ _____I_____ _I__ __.`
AH AZRA VHZMR OTFKRLYFMMB ILRA QH.

21
```
_ _ _ _ N D   _ _ _   _ _ _ _   _ N D   _ _ _ _ _ _ _ _ _ _ :   D _
ZHUHGZ    IRH   SLLX   NGZ   UNIRHXAHQQ:   ZL

_ _ _ _ _ _ _   _ _   _ _ _   _ _ _ _ _ _ _ _ D   _ N D   N _ _ D _ .
DBQIWEH   IL   IRH   NUUAWEIHZ   NGZ   GHHZC.
```

22
```
_ _ _ _ V _   _ _ _ _   _ _   _ _ _ _ _ _ C _   _ _ _
QOYNAO   CQNY   YO   QOZQNULW   URE

C _ _ _ _ _ _ _ ;   _ _ _   _   _ _ V _   _ _ _ _   _ _ _
LNRXOYZX;   CNQ   J   WUAO   MOZX   XWI

_ _ _ _ _ _ _ _ _ _ .
XODXJYNRJOD.
```

23
```
C _ _ _ _ _ _   _ _   _ _   _   _ _ _ _ _   _ _ _ _ _ ,   _   _ _ _ ;
NJZHCZ   GD   BZ   H   NTZHD   EZHJC,   Q   RQU;

_ _ _   _ _ _ _ _   _   _ _ G _ _   _ _ _ _ _ _   _ _ _ _ _ _   _ _ .
HDU   JZDZK   H   JGREC   VSGJGC   KGCEGD   BZ.
```

24
```
_ H _   _ _ _ _ S   _ _   _ H _   H _ _ _ H _ _   _ _ _
BNW   RGSYH   SE   BNW   NWFBNWX   FCW

S _ _ _ _ _   _ _ _   _ _ _ _ ,   _ H _   _ _ _ _   _ _   _ _ _ ' S
HRYJWC   FXG   QSYG,   BNW   KSCV   SE   UWX'H

H _ _ _ S .
NFXGH.
```

25
```
_ _ _ _ V _ _   _ Y   _ _ _ _ ,   _   _ _ _ _ ,   _ _ _ _   _ Y _ _ _
BTHQJTV   WP   AGCH,   G   HGVB,   DVGW   HPQMS

_ _ _ _ ,   _ _ _   _ _ _ _   _   _ _ _ _ _ _ _ _   _ _ _ _ _ _ .
HQOA,   EMB   DVGW   E   BTYTQFDCH   FGMSCT.
```

26

_ GO_, __O_ __O____ __ _OO_____;
G NGZ, XFGM YKGHQLX BJ DGGEVLFKQLL;

___ __ ____ ___ _O_ ___ __O_ ____.
PKZ BJ LVKL PCQ KGX FVZ DCGB XFQQ.

- -

27

___ ___ ___ _S __ _H_ H_____S: H_
ESC NSA MNU JB JH CDT DTZWTHB: DT

H__H ____ _H__S_____ H_ H__H ____S__.
DZCD UNHT QDZCBNTWTA DT DZCD YITZBTU.

- -

28

___ _O__ _____ __ ___ ____: __
SNO DWZL DAHSOSN QF SNO POOI: NO

_____ ___ _____ _O__ _O ___
RCGSOSN SNO VARIOL LWVM SW SNO

__O___.
BZWQML.

- -

29

T___ __ _____, _ ___, ___ ____ ___
NAIV AD ZCZOV, K CKQ, ZVQ FZADG NPS

____ __ _____; ___ __ ___LL __ _____.
BZFG NK DPOVG; ZVQ EG DPZRR XG DZTGQ.

- -

30

___ ___ ___ G___ __ ___ N____N_ ___
MAI CVV FDH UALB AM FDH PCFSAPB CIH

_____: ___ ___ ____ ___ ___ _____N_.
SLAVB: WEF FDH VAIL OCLH FDH DHCRHPB.

31

___ __ ____ __ F___ _F _____: ___
NSD FC XSPT QX NPTT SN UDSPZTLX: BYI

__ __F_ ___W___ ____ ____ ___ _____.
FC TQNL IDBVLUO YQEO PYUS UOL EDBHL.

- -

32

___ ____ _X_____ __G_____ ___
XRP CILH PKPBDXPXR LOSRXPIDQUPQQ GUH

___G____ ___ ___ ____ ___ _____.
MDHSWPUX ZIL GCC XRGX GLP INNLPQQPH.

- -

33

S_ _E___ __ __ ____E_ ___ ___ _, ____
DM FALOS ZD FM UZTHAB MZB XLWD, FSLF

_E ___ _____ ___ _E___ ____ _____.
CA TLW LKKEW MZB SALBFD ZUFM CGDXMT.

- -

34

___ ____ ____ ___ ____: _____ ___ ___
OUK XAYP MTEK OUK FAYP: MYKTO FTN OUK

C_____ __ _____ ____ _U_____ __.
IALQTVB AZ OUANK OUTO QSGXCNUKP CO.

- -

35

___ ___D ____ _____ M_ ____: ___
OIS AJEQ INOI YINROSLSQ US RJES: CMO

__ ____ ___ _____ M_ ____ ____ _____.
IS INOI LJO DFKSL US JKSE MLOJ QSNOI.

36

___ __C___ _____ __ T_____ __T_ ____,
IGD QLSEDT ZGMVV UD IHKPDT LPIA GDVV,

___ ___ T__ __T____ T__T _____T ___.
MPT MVV IGD PMILAPZ IGMI CAKYDI YAT.

37

K____ ___ ____ _____, _ ___: ____
CKKN VDS SQDI RPOKVAK, D WDL: QDOL

___ ___ _____, ___ B_ ___ _____, _
VDS SQZ NKUAK, UVL GK VDS RSPOO, D

_ ___.
WDL.

38

___ _____ ___ ___ _____ _N__ __
IUO LOWWD VQW DIT OUQXL GJDU KT

_____! ___, _____ ___N __N__ __
DVLDW! TWV, LOWWDWQ DIVJ IUJWT DU

__ _____!
KT KUGDI!

39

_____ __N_ _____T ___T_ _____ _N
RTFZL QIYG ALHDOTR XHLRT XLHOU ZY

___N__N__, _N T__ _____ __ T____
IADYGIYMF, ZY RTF MTICAFLU HX RTFZL

__N__.
PZYOU.

40

_ ____, ___ __ W_____ ___ __W
N INWU, KUC TB JNFBOGA LVH MNJ

__W_: ___ __ _____ _____ ___ L___
HNJV: KUC TB RVUUK MUDNFU COU KNFH

___ _____.
NTF WLRUF.

- -

41

_____ __ ___, ___C_ ____ ___ __R___
RITQQTU RT JBU, KODMO OEZO VBZ ZNAVTU

____ __ _R___R, __R ___ __RC_ _R__ __.
EKEH PH FAEHTA, VBA ODQ PTAMH CABP PT.

- -

42

___ ____ _____ ___ _ ___U__ ___ T__
YGP GDXG GDVVI HQP H QPNCXP NMQ YGP

____ ___T_; ___ T__ _____ ___ T__
RDVZ XMHYI; HLZ YGP QMBJI NMQ YGP

_____.
BMLDPI.

- -

43

_____ _R__ _N__R, _N_ __R____ _R___:
YNSRN LJQG SBHNJ, SBP LQJRSFN XJSCA:

_R__ N__ _____ _N _N_ ____ __ __
LJNC BQC CAZRNTL DB SBZ XDRN CQ PQ

____.
NKDT.

44

_ ____, R_____ __ ___ __ __Y _R___:
F AFEU, EBMIXB LB TFJ PT JDC GEZJD:

_____R _____ __ __ __Y ___
TBPJDBE VDZWJBT LB PT JDC DFJ

_____R_.
UPWOABZWIEB.

45

____ __W, _ _____C_ ____, _ ____: _
RJOP IXU, Y GPRPPSQ ZQPP, X KXBC: X

____, _ _____C_ ____, ____ __W
KXBC, Y GPRPPSQ ZQPP, RPIC IXU

_____.
MBXRMPBYZD.

46

___ WO___ O_ ___ _____ ___ _____
OIC UMEPK MH IGK IYBSK YEC ACEGOX

___ _____; ___ ___ _O_____ ___
YBS NZSTVCBO; YJJ IGK QMVVYBSVCBOK YEC

____.
KZEC.

47

L___ __ _ _____ _____ ___
HZGD FL F KFRODJ CZRZDRO OZL

_____, __ ___ L___ _____ ___M
XOZHMJDI, LW ROD HWJM CZRZDRO RODA

____ ____ __M.
ROFR KDFJ OZA.

48

```
_____   ___   ___   _N__   ___   ____;   _R___
BLOODJ   JGX   CUX   VIJL   JGM   RLFA;   JFVTJ

____   _N   ___;   _N_   __   _____   _R_N_   __   __
URTL   DI   GDO;   UIA   GM   TGURR   HFDIS   DJ   JL

____.
EUTT.
```

49

```
T__   ___   ___   ____   B_   _   _____   ___   ___
JNL   EPKG   TERP   XHEE   ZL   T   KLVIYL   VPK   JNL

_____,   _   _____   __   _____   __
POOKLRRLG,   T   KLVIYL   HQ   JHSLR   PV

____B__.
JKPIZEL.
```

50

```
_   _____   ___   ___   _H__   _H_   ____   I_
J   AIDAW   IKR   DWW   AOIA   AOW   MJFR   ED

____:   _____   I_   _H_   ___   _H__
XJJR:   QMWDDWR   ED   AOW   VIK   AOIA

_____ _H   I_   HI_.
AFLDAWAO   EK   OEV.
```

51

```
_E___ _,   __W   ___ _   ___   __W   __E_____
LFJGRW,   JGN   VGGW   QDW   JGN   YRFQAQDB

__   __   ___   __E___E_   __   _WE__   ___E__E_
ZB   ZA   EGU   LUFBJUFD   BG   WNFRR   BGVFBJFU

__   _____!
ZD   HDZBX!
```

52

```
__E ___D __ _____ __, ___ ____ __
KYF IWXC ZB HXREZWNB, RPC GNII WG

_____; ____ __ ___E_, ___ __
EWVMRBBZWP; BIWO KW RPHFX, RPC WG

__E__ _E___.
HXFRK VFXEQ.
```

53

```
_H_ ____ ___S____ _H___ ____ ___;
NMW VFJW ILDEQAWY NMWFJ ZLQDP AWD;

___ _H___ _____S ____ ___ _____ __
KDY NMWFJ AKFYWDE RWJW DLN PFUWD NL

_____.
AKJJFKPW.
```

54

```
__W ____I___ ____ ___ ___ _____
FCT ILYWUCZV NOVC NLY PFJ PFCZKFPV

____ __, _ ___! __W _____ I_ ___ ___
ZGPC XY, C KCB! FCT KLYNP UV PFY VZX

__ ____!
CE PFYX!
```

55

```
__ T___ ____T__, _ G__, _____ T__
CW XLES WYQBXWM, E PEM, QCEKW XLW

_____; __T T__ _____ __ _____ ___
LWQKWIO; BWX XLT PBEHT CW QCEKW QBB

T__ ___T_.
XLW WQHXL.
```

56

_ _ _ _ _   _ _   _ _ _   _ _R_,   _ _ _   _ _ _ _ _ _ _   _ _   _ _
KEYPJ HC JBY AUES, PLS KEYPJAF JU MY

_ _ _ _ _ _ _;   _ _ _   _ _ _   _ _ _ _ _ _ _ _   _ _
WEPHCYS; PLS BHC KEYPJLYCC HC

U_ _ _ _ _ _ _ _ _ _ _ _.
QLCYPEXBPMAY.

- -

57

_   _ _ _ _,   _ _B_ _ _   _ _   _ _ _   I_   _ _I _ _   _ _ _ _ _,
Q RQBJ, BZMHWZ CZ DQL OD LTODZ GDNZB,

_ _I _ _ _ _   _ _ _ _ _ _ _   _ _   I_   _ _ _   _ _ _
DZOLTZB FTGXLZD CZ OD LTA TQL

_ I _ _ _ _ _ _ _ _ _.
JOXIRZGXHBZ.

- -

58

_   _ _ _ _   _ _ _ _ _ _ _ _   _H_   _ _ _ _ _   _ _   _H_   _O_ _:
F KFPP LIRIRVIL AEI KXLJT XO AEI PXLS:

_ _ _ _ _ _   _   _ _ _ _   _ _ _ _ _ _ _ _   _H_   _ _ _ _ _ _ _   _ _
TGLIPB F KFPP LIRIRVIL AEB KXDSILT XO

_ _ _.
XPS.

- -

59

_ _ _ _   _ _ _ _   _ _   _ _ _   F_ _,   _ _ _   _ _ _GG_ _
PGWZ OWWR PI LMC AOI, LMC JPLDDWO

_ _ _ _   _   _ _ _ _ _ _ _   _ _ _,   _ _ _   _ _ _   _ _
RKQW L COXMQWM HLM, LMC LOW LP

_ _ _ _ _   _ _ _ _'   _ _ _.
PGWKO NKPJ' WMC.

60

A_ _
RM BWJ WRIB NRSBJBW RABJI BWJ ORBJI

_ _ _ _ _ _ _, _ _ _ _ _ _ _ _ _ _ _Y _ _ _ _ _ _ _ _ _
UIEEVM, ME NRSBJBW HP MECD RABJI

_ _ _ _, _ _ _ _.
BWJJ, E FET.

- -

61

H_ _ _ _ _ S_ _ _ _ _ _ _ _ _ _ _ _ _ _ _ _ _ _ _S
FW DFUD JZDDWDF ZO DFW FWUTWOJ

S_ _ _ _ _ _ _ _ _ _: _ _ _ _ _ _ _ S_ _ _ _ _ _ _ _ _ _ _ _
JFUXX XUNYF: DFW XPSB JFUXX FUTW DFWE

_ _ _ _ _ _S_ _ _.
ZO BWSZJZPO.

- -

62

_ _ _ _ _ _ _ _ _ _ _U_ U_ _ _ U_, A_ _ _ _ _ _ _
TJB GO XOWNMPQE QDKJ QI, YDB GEOII

U_; A_ _ _AU_ _ _ _ _ _A_ _ _ _ _ _ _ _ U_ _ _
QI; YDB NYQIO CMI PYNO KJ ICMDO QAJD

U_; _ _ _A_.
QI; IOEYC.

- -

63

_ _ _LL _ _ _ _ _E _ _E _ _ _E _ _ _ _ _ _ _ _ _ _
S VSKK JOUSBH RZH WULH YT CYQ VSRZ U

_ _ _ _, _ _ _ _ _LL _ _ _ _ _ _ _ _ _ _ _ _ _
BYWC, UWQ VSKK LUCWSTP ZSL VSRZ

_ _ _ _ _ _ _ _ _ _ _ _ _.
RZUWGBCSESWC.

64

```
___ _H_ H_____, _ ____, ___ __M_
DNU PZR ZAOSAHV, N TNIG, OHG KNXA

____: ____H _H_ M_____, ___ _H__
GNUH: PNCKZ PZA XNCHPOJHV, OHG PZAR

_H___ _M___.
VZOTT VXNFA.
```

65

```
__ _____ ___ W_____SS ____ _
ZY BGAVYBZ BZY KQXHYAVYCC QVBE D

S_____ W____, ___ ___ _____ ____
CBDVHQVS KDBYA, DVH HAN SAEGVH QVBE

W____S_____S.
KDBYACIAQVSC.
```

66

```
__, _____N ___ _N _____ __ ___
SL, KGXSHCNM ECN EM GNCXOEBN LQ OGN

____: _N_ ___ ____ __ ___ W___ __
SLCH: EMH OGN QCPXO LQ OGN VLDY XJ

___ __W___.
GXJ CNVECH.
```

67

```
_____G_ ___ __ ____ __ ___I_____:
VKGWMNK NWB RD CKTSS BW YTSQTIVSO:

___ __ I_ I_ ____ _____ _____ ____
UWG KD QV QC VKTV CKTSS VGDTB BWRI

___ ____I__.
WMG DIDEQDC.
```

68

`__  ____  _____  W___  ___  _____,  W_`
QO BNTO PXEEOY QXAB LWU KNABOUP, QO

`____  _____  _____,  W_  ____`
BNTO SLHHXAAOY XEXDWXAV, QO BNTO

`____  W__K____.`
YLEO QXSCOYRV.

69

`B__  ____,  O  _O__,  _____  _____  __  ____;`
ATF FICT, C DCYK, JIVDF DVTRI VF FIGN;

`____  _____  ____  ___  ___  _____  __`
FICT JIVDF IVBG VDD FIG IGVFIGP EP

`_____.`
KGYEJECP.

70

`___  T_E  ____  ____  __T  ___T  ___  ___`
DVT JLG EVTK BYEE RVJ NOFJ VDD LYF

`_E___E,  _E_T_E_  ____  _E  _____E  ___`
WGVWEG, RGYJLGT BYEE LG DVTFOUG LYF

`___E__T___E.`
YRLGTYJORNG.

71

`_____  ___  ____  __R  ___,  ___  __R____`
JCRNV VFJ NYHX YSH DYX, RLX EYHQFAI

`__  ___  ____  ____;  F_R  ___  ____  __R`
RV FAQ FYNK FANN; MYH VFJ NYHX YSH

`___  __  ____.`
DYX AQ FYNK.

72

```
__  ____  _ _ _ _ _ _,  _ _R D,  __  _ _ _ _ _  ___
CP  JFUS  PWHRJPM,  RUQM,  VA  JFVAP  UOA

_____:  __  ____  __  ____  ___  _____
IJQPAKJF:  IU  OVRR  OP  IVAK  HAM  YQHVIP

___  _____.
JFD  YUOPQ.
```

73

```
_____T  T_Y____  ____  __  T__  ____;  ___
HVALUPO  OPRZVAI  JAZT  LX  OPV  ATGH;  JXH

__  _____  ____  T___  T__  _____  __
PV  ZPJAA  ULEV  OPVV  OPV  HVZLGVZ  TI

T____  ____T.
OPLXV  PVJGO.
```

74

```
___  _N___  __  ___  ____  _N___P___
BTY  XPOYN  HQ  BTY  NHWC  YPRXGMYBT

_ __N_  _____  ___  ___  ___  ___,  _N_
WHVPC  XZHVB  BTYG  BTXB  QYXW  TEG,  XPC

_____  ____.
CYNEKYWYBT  BTYG.
```

75

```
T__  ____  _____;  ___  B_____  B_  __
FBM  GCWH  GUDMFB;  EQH  YGMIIMH  YM  SN

_ _C_;  ___  ___  ___  ___  __  __
WCJT;  EQH  GMF  FBM  OCH  CR  SN

_____  B_  _____.
IEGDEFUCQ  YM  MZEGFMH.
```

76

```
_ _ _ _ _ _ _ _ _ _ _ _   _ _ _   _ _ _ _ _ _ _ _ _ _ _ _, _ _ _V_
A G W A D I W T W N   S P C   S D O S T K G W T D O,  T  P L Q D

_ _ _ _ _   _ _   _ L _   _ _ _ _   _ _ _ _   _ _ _ _   _ _ _ _ _ _ _
M W G H W   G U   G J B   S P L S   S P G Z   P L O S   U G Z W B D B

_ _ _ _   _ _ _   _ V _ _.
S P D K   U G I   D Q D I.
```

77

```
_ _ _ _   _ _   _ O   _ N _ _ _ _ _ N _   _ _ _   _ _ _   O _   _ _ _
U L N Q   U Q   I A   V R T Q D B I L R T   I F Q   K L Z   A Y   I F Z

_ _ _ _ _ _ _ _:  _ O   _ _ _ _ _   _   _ _ _ _   O _   _ _ _
J D Q M Q J I B:  B A   B F L E E   C   I L E N   A Y   I F Z

_ O N _ _ O _ _   _ O _ _ _.
K A R T D A V B   K A D N B.
```

78

```
_ _ _   _ _ _   _ _ _ _ _ _ _ _ _   _ _ R _   _ _ V _ _ _
T X N   D U C   N F H U D C X B I   O X N J   O X M C D U

_ _ _ _ _ _ _ _ _ _ _ _ _;   _ _ _   _ _ _ _ _ _ _ _ _ _   _ _ _ _
N F H U D C X B I P C I I;   U F I   G X B P D C P K P G C   J X D U

_ _ _ _ _ _   _ _ _   _ _ _ _ _ _ _.
Y C U X O J   D U C   B R N F H U D.
```

79

```
F _ _   _ _ _   _ _ _ D   _ _ _ _ _ _   _ _ _ _ _ _ _ _   _ _   _ _ _
E I P   O K W   U I P C   O V S W O K   L U W V Z M P W   G R   K G Z

_ _ _ _ _ _:  _ _   _ _ _ _   _ _ _ _ _ _ _ _   _ _ _   _ _ _ _
L W I L U W:  K W   H G U U   F W V M O G E A   O K W   B W W S

_ _ _ _   _ _ _ _ _ _ _ _ _.
H G O K   Z V U Q V O G I R.
```

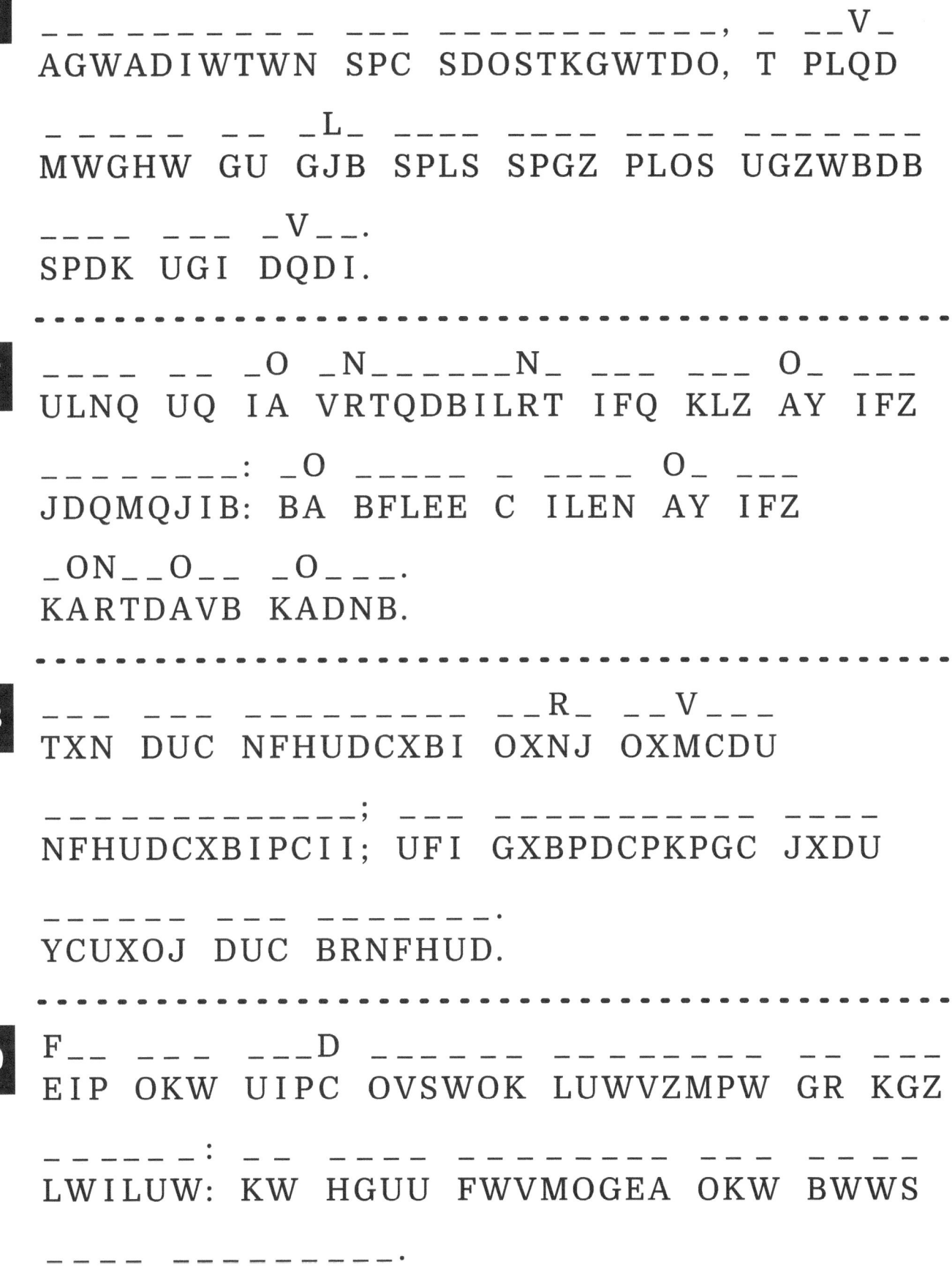

80

P _ _ _ C _ _   _ _ _ _   _ _ _ _ _ C _ _ _ _   _ _   _ _ _ _ _ _ _   _
ZKFALPC YGWP ZPKCPLHQPV IP TFQYEHQ G

C _ _ _ _ _: _ _ _   _ _   _ _ _ _ _   _ _ _ _ _ _ _ _   _ _   _ _ _
LGHCP: XHQ IU YPGKQ CQGAVPQY FA GTP

_ _   _ _ _   _ _ _ _.
EO QYU TEKV.

- -

81

_   _ _ _ _   _ _ _   O _   _ _ _   _ _ _ _,   _ _   _ _   M _
H VHJJ UBW FK PYC JFOL, YC HU SW

_ _ _ _ _ _   _ _ _   M _   _ O _ _ _ _ _ _: M _   _ O _;   _ _
OCKQMC BEL SW KFOPOCUU: SW MFL; HE

_ _ M   _ _ _ _   _   _ _ _ _ _.
YHS VHJJ H POQUP.

- -

82

_   _ _ _ _   P _ A _ _ _   _ _ _ _,   _   _ _ _ _,   A _ _ _ _   _ _ _
D BDMM QVWDFI HCII, T MTVP, WRTSJ HCI

P _ _ P _ _: _   _ _ _ _   _ _ _ _   _ _ _ _   _ _ _ _   A _ _ _ _
QITQMI: D BDMM FDSJ ASHT HCII WRTSJ

_ _ _   _ A _ _ _ _ _.
HCI SWHDTSF.

- -

83

_ _ _ _   _ N _   _ _ _   _ H _   _ _ _ _ _   _ _   _ _ _: H _   _ _
LXID MKE JDD AVD TXOPJ XQ ZXE: VD HJ

_ _ _ _ _ _ _ _   _ N   H _ _   _ _ _ N _   _ _ _ _ _ _   _ H _
ADOOHSFD HK VHJ EXHKZ AXTMOE AVD

_ H _ _ _ _ _ N   _ _   _ _ N.
LVHFEODK XQ IDK.

84

```
_O__   ___   ____,   __ _ __   ____   ____      GO_,
PUXK   TMN   RKTV,   TWW  IK    DRTD   GKTV      SUN,

___ _ ____    _____    ____ __  ____
TMN F ZFWW   NKPWTVK    ZRTD RK  RTDR

_O__ _O_ __ _O__.
NUMK GUV XI QUEW.
```

85

```
__   __T_   __T   ____T   __T_   __   _FT__   ___
QW   QFLQ   SZL   IWFYL   DULQ   VB   FOLWT   ZVT

____;   ___   _____   __   _____   T_   ___
BUSB;   SZT   TWDFTIWI   VB   FGGZTIUSN   LZ   ZVT

_____T____.
USUEVULUWB.
```

86

```
__   G___,   _   ____,   __T_   T____   T__T   __
TN   PNNT,   N   QNST,   VBKN   KCNLW   KCHK   FW

G___,   ___   T_   T___   T__T   ___   ____G_T
PNNT,   HBT   KN   KCWU   KCHK   HSW   VGSRPCK

__   T____   ___ __T_.
RB   KCWRS   CWHSKL.
```

87

```
____E   ____   _E   ____ _E_   __   __E   ____E
KXENI   KXQK   DI   GVQWKIJ   HW   KXI   XEBNI

__   __E   __R_   _____   _____   __   __E
EM   KXI   VEAJ   NXQVV   MVEBAHNX   HW   KXI

_____   __   ___ ___.
ZEBAKN   EM   EBA   TEJ.
```

88

```
_O_ ___ ____ __O____ ___ ___ O_ ___
BKE MAO XKEZ YCKJOMA MAO JIP KB MAO
```

```
_____O__: ___ ___ ___ O_ ___
ENDAMOKSF: LSM MAO JIP KB MAO
```

```
___OD__ _____ _____.
SCDKZXP FAIXX QOENFA.
```

89

```
__R T___ ___T ____T_____ __ R___T ___
WLQ EPLY PTUE OTZRETZRJG ON QZFPE TRG
```

```
__ _____; T___ __T__T __ T__ T_R___
ON KTYUJ; EPLY UTEJUE ZR EPJ EPQLRJ
```

```
_____ R___T.
IYGFZRF QZFPE.
```

90

```
____ ___ _S __ ____ _____ ___ ___D?
QBSV YSC PZ BH VBSV THSUHVB VBH KWUR?
```

```
___ S____ __ _____ __ ___ ___ ____ __
BPY ZBSKK BH VHSDB PC VBH QSL VBSV BH
```

```
S____ ___ _S_.
ZBSKK DBWWZH.
```

91

```
___ _HE ____ __ ____; H__ _E___ __
GCX SNB FCXI OT UCCI; NOT RBXYP OT
```

```
E_E_____; ___ H__ ____H E____E_H
BKBXFWTSOEU; WEI NOT SXQSN BEIQXBSN
```

```
__ ___ _E_E_____.
SC WFF UBEBXWSOCET.
```

92

```
____ ____ ___     _O_D ___ _____ ___ ____
DECK TQLP LBK MPOJ LBK DMPOZ JTK TQLP

___ _A__; _____ ___ _O_D __ ___
BEA QHWK; FPOABEU LBK MPOJ EQ LBK

__A___ __ _____.
NKHTLZ PY BPMEQKAA.
```

93

```
_ _A__ ___ ___ L___ A__A__ B_____ __:
M BRXL ULG GBL VKEP RVQRJU SLDKEL OL:

B__A___ __ __ A_ __ _____ _A__, _
SLHRFUL BL MU RG OJ EMTBG BRZP, M

__A__ ___ B_ _____.
UBRVV ZKG SL OKXLP.
```

94

```
___U, ____ ___U, ___ __ __ F_____: ___
RJQK, OEOB RJQK, FIR RQ CO AOFIOH: FBH

___ ___ _____ __ ___ _____ ____ ____
PJQ SFZ XRFBH NB RJZ XNLJR PJOB QBVO

___U ___ _____?
RJQK FIR FBLIZ?
```

95

```
_R__ T__ R_____ __ T__ ___ __T_ T__
MXGP CJL XSYSEI GM CJL YFE FECG CJL

_____ ____ __ T__ ____ T__ ____'_ ____
IGSEI BGRE GM CJL YNPL CJL QGXB'Y ENPL

__ T_ __ _R_____.
SY CG WL DXNSYLB.
```

96

```
_____A_  __A__  A  _____  MA_
VUFAFVBJUWP  YUWPP  W  XZNKM  LWK

___A___  ___  _A_?  __  _A____  ____
DPFWKYF  UBY  VWX?  EX  JWRBKM  UFFS

_____  A_____  __  ___  ____.
JUFAFJZ  WDDZASBKM  JZ  JUX  VZAS.
```

97

```
__  _____T_T_  __T  __  T__  _T____T_  __
BA  GAEOQBXAXB  VSX  OV  XBA  DXPAVQXB  SZ

T__  _____:  __  T___T_  __T  _____U__  __
XBA  BSPDA:  BA  XTWAXB  VSX  LEATDYPA  OV

T__  ____  __  _  ___.
XBA  EAQD  SZ  T  KTV.
```

98

```
_____E  _HE  ____  ___H  H___:  ____  ____
ZGYDEO  RBO  APGU  IDRB  BYGZ:  EDMF  TMRP

H__  ___H  _HE  _____E__  ___  __
BDV  IDRB  RBO  ZEYAROGX  YMU  YM

_____E__  __  _E_  _____.
DMERGTVOMR  PK  ROM  ERGDMFE.
```

99

```
_Y  _____  ___  _Y  __R_  _____:  ___
QB  UHKDT  ICE  QB  TKILM  UIFHKMT:  WRM

___  __  ___  __R_____  __  _Y  __R_,  ___
JSE  FD  MTK  DMLKCJMT  SU  QB  TKILM,  ICE

_Y  __R____  __R  ___R.
QB  VSLMFSC  USL  KAKL.
```

100

```
___U S____   __S____   ____  ____   S____
QPTD CPZEQ   OKCQSTU   QPKL  QPZQ    CFKZW

___S_ ___:   ___  _O__  ____  _____  ___
EKZCHMJ: QPK ETSO GHEE ZRPTS QPK

_____  ___  _____U_ ___.
RETTOU ZMO OKVKHQADE LZM.
```

101

```
____,  __O_  __S_  ____  ___O_____  ___O
YNOI,  MRNF  RDTM  HUUG  BDLNFODHYU  FGMN

___  ____:  __O_  __S_  __O____  __C_
MRJ  YDGI:  MRNF  RDTM  HONFXRM  HDWV

___  C_____  O_  __CO_.
MRU  WDZMALAMJ  NB  SDWNH.
```

102

```
__  O__  H___  _HO_  ____  _H_
MR  MPC  ONJH  HOMF  PNKC  HOU

_O_____O_  O_  _H_  ____H:  ___  _H_
RMFXCNHKMX  MR  HOU  UNWHO:  NXC  HOU

H_____  ___  _H_  _O__  O_  _H_  H____.
OUNTUXJ  NWU  HOU  SMWQ  MR  HOG  ONXCJ.
```

103

```
_  ____,  _  ___D,  T__T  T_Y  _____T_
M  BIUH,  U  WUNK,  CFZC  CFO  QTKDLJICR

___  ____T,  ___  T__T  T___  __
ZNJ  NMDFC,  ZIK  CFZC  CFUT  MI

___T_____  ___T  _____ _T__  __.
XZMCFXTWIJRR  FZRC  ZXXWMGCJK  LJ.
```

104

```
_ _ _ _   _ _ _ S _   _ _   _H_ _ _ _ _ S,   _ _ _   S _ _ _   _ _
MRCB  WDTMW  YK  NFSDYRWM,  SKL  MRCB  YK
```

```
H _ _ S _ S:   _ _ _   _ _   _ _ _ _   _ _ _ _ _ _ _ _   _H_
FRDMBM:  XTW  VB  VYUU  DBCBCXBD  WFB
```

```
_ _ _ _   _ _   _H_   _ _ _ _   _ _ _   _ _ _.
KSCB  RJ  WFB  URDL  RTD  HRL.
```

105

```
_ _ _   _ _ _ _ _ _   _ _ _   _ _ _ _ _ _ _ _ _   _ _O_   _ _ _
GSZ  VCTAZM  JQZ  ZBGQJOFZM  XQEP  GSZ
```

```
_O_ _:   _ _ _ _   _O   _ _ _ _ _ _   _ _   _OO_   _ _   _ _ _ _
VEPW:  GSZK  FE  JBGQJK  JB  BEEO  JB  GSZK
```

```
_ _   _O_ _,   _ _ _ _ _ _ _ _   L _ _ _.
WZ  WEQO,  BIZJACOF  RCZB.
```

106

```
_ _ _   _ _ _   _ _ _   _ _O_   _ _ _ _   _ _O_,   _ _O_ _
WLSW  XDV  XSP  TVBM  WLSW  WLBA,  MLBRD
```

```
_ _ _ _   _ _O_ _   _ _   _ _ _ _ _ _ _,   _R_   _ _ _   _O_ _
VSXD  SCBVD  HR  EDLBGSL,  SQW  WLD  XBRW
```

```
_ _ _ _   O _ _R   _ _ _   _ _ _   _ _R _ _.
LHKL  BGDQ  SCC  WLD  DSQWL.
```

107

```
_ _ _ _ _ _ _   _ _   _ _ _ _ _ _ _   _ _ _ _   G _ _:   _ _ _
NZDYJIL  XL  ZHYLMPHS  BMHC  PCE:  SJZ
```

```
_ _ _ _ _ _ _ _ _   _ _   _ _ _ _   I _ _ _ _ _,   _ _ _   _ _ _
LWDLVVLMDX  JZ  CGLY  JZYNLV,  NME  SJZ
```

```
_ _ _ _ _ _ _ _   _ _   _ _   _ _ _   _ _ _ _ _ _.
ZHYLMPHS  JZ  JM  HSL  DVCBEZ.
```

108

```
_ _ _ _   _ _ _   _ _ _ _ _ _ _   _ _ _ _U_ _   _ _
CUDH  WPH  HFEBDQC  TDVKRBD  PC

_ _ _ _ D _ _ _ _ _,   _ _ _ _ _ _ _   _ _   _ _ _U   _ _ _ _ _U_
DYNQMPDUB,  WDNHFDU  TD  HFPR  DWYNPRB

_ _ _ _ _ _ _   _ _ _   _ _ _ _ _ _ _   _ _   _ _ _ _U_ _ _.
KJKNWBH  HFD  SPUODUB  PC  NWNLRNHE.
```

109

```
_ _ _ _ _ _   _ _ _   _ _ _ _   _ _   _ _ _ _,   Y_ _   _ _ _ _   _ _
NQKTIQ  NQJ  PKWH  ZJ  QBIQ,  DJN  QRNQ  QJ

_ _ _ _ _C_   _ _ _ _   _ _ _   L_ _LY:   _ _ _   _ _ _
WJCVJUN  TGNK  NQJ  PKEPD:  ZTN  NQJ

_ _ _ _ _   _ _   _ _ _ _ _ _   _ _ _ _   _ _ _.
VWKTH  QJ  LGKEJNQ  RXRW  KXX.
```

110

```
_ _E_   _ _E_R   _ _ _ _E_   _RE   _ _ER_ _R_ _ _   _ _
EGIU  HGILD  SQBMIK  TDI  CZIDHGDCEU  LU

_ _ _ _ _   _ _ _ _E_,   _ _E_   _ _ _ _ _   _E_R   _ _
KHCUF  JXTVIK,  HGIF  KGTXX  GITD  YF

_ _R_ _;   _ _R   _ _E_   _RE   _ _EE_.
ECDBK;  WCD  HGIF  TDI  KEIIH.
```

111

```
_   H_ _   _ _ _N_ _ _,   _N_ _ _ _   _   H_ _   _ _ _ _ _ _ _ _ _
Z  BPV  TPZHXNV,  DHKNRR  Z  BPV  GNKZNWNV

_ _   _ _ _   _H_   _ _ _ _N_ _ _   _ _   _H_   _ _ _ _   _N
XS  RNN  XBN  ASSVHNRR  ST  XBN  KSCV  ZH

_H_   _ _N_   _ _   _H_   _ _ _ _N_.
XBN  KPHV  ST  XBN  KZWZHA.
```

112

```
__  __T_  _____  ___  _____T F__
BS  BFUB  ISZSZASISH  BKC  VMQSPFPU NMI

____,  T__  ____  _____  __  _____ T_
SQSI, UBS  OMIH  OBKVB  BS  VMZZFPHSH UM

_ T_____  _____T____.
F UBMTCFPH  YSPSIFUKMPC.
```

113

```
___  ____  __  ____  ____  ___  B_____:
SEQ  CLBY  NP  SBDK  JBLH  SEK  RKVNMMNMV:

___  _V___  ___  __  ___  _____
FMY  KXKBQ  LMK  LJ  SEQ  BNVESKLDP

_____  _____  ___  _V__.
GDYVHKMSP  KMYDBKSE  JLB  KXKB.
```

114

```
L__  _S  ____  _____  __S  ___S____  ____
KYB  AF  UDNY  PYEDZY  LMF  OZYFYCUY  VMBL

____S_____,  ___  ____  _  _____  ___S_
BLTCQFHMRMCH,  TCG  NTQY  T  XDSEAK  CDMFY

____  ___  ____  _S___S.
ACBD  LMN  VMBL  OFTKNF.
```

115

```
___  ___  _____  __  ___  ____  ___
EWW  XTB  CEXTV  HZ  XTB  WHMQ  EMB

M____  ___  _____  ____  ____  __  ____
 IBMRD  EUQ  XMOXT  OUXH  VORT  EV  GBBC

___  __V____  ___  ___  _____M_____.
TYV  RHKBUEUX  EUQ  TYV  XBVXYI HUYBV.
```

116

```
I _ ____ ___ _E _____ __ _E_ _____
U AUGG RBY PS IONIUC BO YSR YVBMEIRCE
__ _E___E, ____ ___E _E_ __E__E__E_
BO XSBXGS, YVIY VIHS ESY YVSLESGHSE
_____ _E _____ _____.
IJIUREY LS NBMRC IPBMY.
```

117

```
__ ___ _____ _ __P_____ T_ ___
AV XJV SVDPEV X JVOJPXDU BP PHJ
_____, _ _____ ___ _____ T_
GVCMUSPHJR, X RDPJG XGL LVJCRCPG BP
T___ T__T ___ _____ ____T __.
BUVE BUXB XJV JPHGL XSPHB HR.
```

118

```
___ _____ __ ___ ____ ___ ____
UMV HBQXO BZ UMV CBQX IQV YFQV
_____: __ _____ _____ __ _ _____C_
HBQXO: IO OKCJVQ UQKVX KA I ZFQAINV
__ _____, _____ _____ __M__.
BZ VIQUM, YFQKZKVX OVJVA UKTVO.
```

119

```
___R___R_ _ __T___ ___ T__ _R____T_
KIPVPAHVP Z PRKPPY TDD KIW BVPLPBKR
_____R____ ___ T_____ T_ __ R___T; ___
LHJLPVJZJF TDD KIZJFR KH UP VZFIK; TJS
_ __T_ ___R_ _____ ___.
Z ITKP PCPVW ATDRP ETW.
```

120

```
_ _ E   _ _ _ D   _ _   _ _ _ _   _ _   _ _ _ _ _ _ _ E _   _ _ _ _   _ _ E
B O C   X V F E   V Y   O A R O   A K   I A R O B A C F   B O H Y   B O C
```

```
_ _ _ _ E   _ _   _ _ _ _   _ _ _ E _ _ ,   _ E _ ,   _ _ _ _   _ _ E
Y V A K C   V J   I H Y N   T H B C F K ,   N C H ,   B O H Y   B O C
```

```
_ _ _ _ _ _   _ _ _ E _   _ _   _ _ E   _ E _ .
I A R O B N   T H L C K   V J   B O C   K C H .
```

- -

121

```
_ O _   T _ O _   _ _ _ _ T   _ _ T   T _ _   _ _ _ O _ _   O _
A T O   Q X T Y   L X R P Q   F R Q   Q X F   P R K T Y O   T A
```

```
T _ _ _ _   _ _ _ _ _ :   _ _ _ _ _   _ _ _ _ T   T _ O _   _ _ ,   _ _ _
Q X Z E F   X R E V L :   X R S S U   L X R P Q   Q X T Y   K F ,   R E V
```

```
_ T   _ _ _ _ _   _ _   _ _ _ _   _ _ T _   T _ _ _ .
Z Q   L X R P P   K F   I F P P   I Z Q X   Q X F F .
```

- -

122

```
_ _ _   _ _ _ _   _ _   _ _ _ _   _ _ _ _   _ _ _ _   _ _ _ _   _ _ _
X V P   W Y D E   O F   M O T V   Q M X Y   X V P Z   X V C X   C D P
```

```
_ F   _   _ _ _ _ _ _   _ _ _ _ _ ;   _ _ D   _ _ _ _ _ _   _ _ _ _   _ _
Y J   C   A D Y L P M   V P C D X ;   C M E   F C U P X V   F Q I V   C F
```

```
_ _   _ F   _   _ _ _ _ _ _ _ _   _ _ _ _ _ _ .
A P   Y J   C   I Y M X D O X P   F H O D O X .
```

- -

123

```
_ _ _ T   T _ _ _   _ _ _ _ T   _ _ T   T _ _ _ _   _ _ _ _   _ _   _ _ _ ,
Q C R Q   Q C P K   Z V Y C Q   E P Q   Q C P V J   C U T P   V O   Y U F ,
```

```
_ _ _   _ _ T   _ _ _ _ _ T   T _ _   _ _ _ K _   _ _   _ _ _ ,   _ _ T
R O F   O U Q   M U J Y P Q   Q C P   A U J G E   U M   Y U F ,   N X Q
```

```
K _ _ _   _ _ _   _ _ _ _ _ _ _ _ _ _ T _ :
G P P T   C V E   I U Z Z R O F Z P O Q E :
```

124

```
_ _ _ _ _ E _   _ E ,   _   _ _ _ _ ,   _ _ _   _ _ _   _ _ _ E ' _
P D U T R Z F   L Z ,   K   E K A W ,   J K A   M G X   F Y L Z ' V

_ _ _ E :   _ _ _   _ _ _   _ _ _ _ _ E _ _ _ _ E _ _ '   _ _ _ E
V Y R Z :   J K A   M G X   A U C G M Z K D V F Z V V '   V Y R Z

_ _ _ _ _   _ _   _ _ _ L   _ _ _   _ _   _ _ _ _ _ L E .
S A U F C   L X   V K D E   K D M   K J   M A K D S E Z .
```

125

```
_ _   _ _ _   _ _ _ _   _ _   _ _ _   _ _ _ _   _ _ _ _   _ _ _
A O   H Y W   D E V U   E I   H Y W   J E V U   D W V W   H Y W

_ _ _ _ _ _ _   _ _ _ _ ;   _ _ _   _ _ _   _ _ _   _ _ _ _   _ _
Y W B T W S P   F B U W ;   B S U   B J J   H Y W   Y E P H   E I

_ _ _ _   B _   _ _ _   B _ _ _ _ _   _ _   _ _ _   _ _ U _ _ .
H Y W F   A O   H Y W   A V W B H Y   E I   Y Q P   F E K H Y .
```

126

```
_ _   _ _ _ _   _ _ _ _ _ _ _ _   _ _   _ _ _   _ _ _ _ _ _   _ _ _ _ _
E P   Y E D Y   J U P G G P Y E   W M   Y E P   N P I H P Y   S G D I P

_ _   _ _ _   M _ _ _   _ _ _ _   _ _ _ _ _   _ B _ _ _   _ _ _ _ _
V Q   Y E P   Z V N Y   E W K E   N E D G G   D X W J P   A M J P H

_ _ _   _ _ _ _ _ _   _ _   _ _ _   _ _ M _ _ _ _ _ .
Y E P   N E D J V U   V Q   Y E P   D G Z W K E Y L .
```

127

```
_ _ _   _ _ _ _ _ _   _ _ _ _   _ _   _ _ _   _ O _ _ :   _ _ _   _ _ _ _
Z B X   A F N S B Z   C Q J B   A T   X C B   Z Q N Y :   H Q N   V A X C

_ _ _   _ O _ _   _ _ _ _ _   _ _   _ _ _ _ _ ,   _ _ D   _ _ _ _   _ _ _
X C B   Z Q N Y   X C B N B   A F   E B N I L ,   S T Y   V A X C   C A E

_ _   _ _ _ _ _ _ _ _ _   _ _ D _ _ _ _ _ _ .
A F   J Z B T X B Q K F   N B Y B E J X A Q T .
```

128

```
__  ____T_  T__  __RR__  _____    T_  ____
QP  XHBPAQ  AQP  EHSSPF  IWXHF  AW  BPPJ

_____,  ___   T_  __  _  _____  __T__R  __
QWMRP,  HFO  AW  EP  H  VWNZMK  XWAQPS  WZ

__I__R__.  _R_I__  __  T__  ____.
GQLKOSPF.  JSHLRP  NP  AQP  KWSO.
```

129

```
___  _  ___U____  _____  __  ___  _____
MAJ  H  GCAIDHVR  LYHJD  EV  GCL  DEBCG

___  _U_  __  _____  W___  __  __  ____,
HJY  XIG  HD  LYDGYJRHL  PCYV  EG  ED  OHDG,

___  __  _  W____  __  ___  _____.
HVR  HD  H  PHGNC  EV  GCY  VEBCG.
```

130

```
_A__  __  ___  L___:  __  __  ____  ____A__,
UYKI  QB  IEZ  NQOA:  PZ  QM  SQQA  FQXOYSZ,

A__  __  __A__  _____  _____  __A__:
YBA  EZ  CEYNN  CIOZBSIEZB  IEKBZ  EZYOI:

_A__,  _  _A_,  __  ___  L___.
UYKI,  K  CYW,  QB  IEZ  NQOA.
```

131

__ ____ __ ___ ____, ___ _____, Y_
IJ MDSL KG PQJ DUOL, SGL OJBUKYJ, RJ

_ _ _ _ _ _ _U_: ___ ___U_ ___ __Y, ___ Y_
OKMQPJUAC: SGL CQUAP WUO BUR, SDD RJ

____ ___ U_____ __ _____.
PQSP SOJ AFOKMQP KG QJSOP.

132

C_____ ___ _____ ___ _____ _____
IVZOPK JTP PJQUTGKK JQG QZOTP JYZOF

___: __G_____ ___ ___G____ ___
DLR: QLMDFGZOKTGKK JTP BOPMRGTF JQG

___ _____ __ ___ _____.
FDG DJYLFJFLZT ZS DLK FDQZTG.

133

____ __RR___ _____ __ __ ___ _____:
LJKX FDZZDTF FBJOO MW ND NBW TRAVWI:

_U_ __ ____ _RU____ __ ___ ____,
MQN BW NBJN NZQFNWNB RK NBW ODZI,

_ _R__ _____ _____ ___ ___U_.
LWZAX FBJOO ADLGJFF BRL JMDQN.

134

`__ ___ _ ____ _____ ___ ____, __ ___`
DI TNK D VDRR XYFDCZ UDC VNYK, DI TNK

`_ ____ ___ _Y _____; _ ____ ___ ____`
D UFHZ XSA JB AYSCA; D VDRR INA MZFY

`____ _____ C__ __ ____ __.`
VUFA MRZCU QFI KN SIAN JZ.

- -

135

`___I___ __, _ __ ___, ___ __ ___ ____`
LXQHKXD RX, I RV MIL, IOC IT CJX JFBL

`__ ___ _I____, ___ __ ___ ____ __ ___`
IT CJX AHESXL, IOC IT CJX JFBL IT CJX

`___I_____S ___ _____ ___.`
OBDHMJCXIOZ FBL EDOXQ RFB.

- -

136

`__ ___ _ ____ ____, _ ____, ____ ____`
FJ SJR C GQRH RGHE, J KJWF, RGQR GQRH

`____? ___ __ ___ _ _____ ____`
RGHH? QSF QE SJR C NWCHAHF DCRG

`___S_ ____ __S_ _P _____S_ ____?`
RGJBH RGQR WCBH TM QNQCSBR RGHH?

137

`__ ___LL, __D ____ ____ _ __ __D: _`
VT AMKSS, RZG UZDF MXRM K RO LDG: K

`__LL __ ___L__D _____ ___ _____, _`
FKSS VT TQRSMTG RODZL MXT XTRMXTZ, K

`__LL __ ___L__D __ ___ _____.`
FKSS VT TQRSMTG KZ MXT TRIMX.

- -

138

`__ ____ _____ __ __T_____ __ __T_`
EX TRLI TSBII QY TBCKTGKYZ BT OKCS

`M_____ ___ __T____; ___ M_ M__T_`
EBMMRO BVZ GBCVYTT; BVZ EX ERLCS

`_____ _____ T___ __T_ _____ ____:`
TSBII NMBKTY CSYY OKCS WRXGLI IKNT:

- -

139

`__R ____ __ ____P__ __ _ __R_ ___ __`
IVO UIVY ZU AUNMFAK MU M XZOK IVG IS

`___ ___R_ __ ___ _____R_: ___ ___R_`
GLA UCMOA IS GLA SIRYAOU: GLA UCMOA

`__ _R____, ___ __ _R_ ____P__.`
ZU XOITAC, MCK RA MOA AUNMFAK.

140

_ ____, ___ ___I____ ___ ___ _____! I_
J ZJSH, DJB NGVXUJZH GSO IDK BJSLC! XV

_I____ ____ ____ ____ ____ ___: ___
BXCHJN DGCI IDJT NGHO IDON GZZ: IDO

_____ I_ ____ __ ___ _IC___.
OGSID XC UTZZ JU IDK SXQDOC.

141

___ _____ __ G_D ___ _ _____
LOR WYAKTDTARW ND CNI YKR Y JKNZRH

_ _____: _ _____ __D _ _____
WMTKTL: Y JKNZRH YHI Y ANHLKTLR

_____, _ G_D, ____ ____ ___ D_____.
ORYKL, N CNI, LONS GTXL HNL IRWMTWR.

142

_____ __ ___ N____N _____ ___ __
VOYNNYU HN DQY SRDHTS EQTNY ITU HN

___ _____; _N_ ___ _____ ____ __ ____
DQY OTBU; RSU DQY JYTJOY EQTL QY QRDQ

_____N __R ___ __N _N__R___N__.
MQTNYS KTB QHN TES HSQYBHDRSMY.

143

```
__O_O __ ____,  ___ ____  O_____
ISCPC BP IBPW,  TKJ IBXX  CMPWQYW

_____ ____G_,  ____ ____ _____
VSWPW VSBKFP,  WYWK VSWH PSTXX

_____ ___ _O___G_____ O_ ___
ZKJWQPVTKJ VSW XCYBKFABKJKWPP CR VSW

____.
XCQJ.
```

144

```
_ ____ __ __ ___ _____ __ ___
E VEQQ TR EL NWY GNSYLTNW RB NWY

____ G__:  _ ____ ____ _____ __ ___
QRSC TRC:  E VEQQ PIXY PYLNERL RB NWA

_____U_____,  ____ __ _____ ____.
SETWNYRZGLYGG,   YHYL RB NWELY RLQA.
```

145

```
__ _R_____ ____ F_R__ ____ ____
OR JADLIOX XORV NDAXO SWBD UTXO

_____R ___ ____:  ___ ___R_ ___ ___
BTWFRA SPC IDWC:  SPC XORAR USB PDX

___ F_____ __R___ _____ ____R _R____.
DPR NRRJWR QRABDP SVDPI XORTA XATJRB.
```

146

```
F__ ____, ____, ___ ____, ___ _____ __
SFG AWFN, IFGM, TGA XFFM, TPM GVTMC AF

____I__; ___ _____ I_ _____ ____
SFGXOYV; TPM KIVPAVFNZ OP LVGQC NPAF

___ ____ ____ ____ ____ ____.
TII AWVL AWTA QTII NKFP AWVV.
```

147

```
T__ _____, _____ ___ _____ __ ___
RZO FBYJOL, RZHWTSZ RZO DHBLO WV ZBI

_ _____ ___, __LL ___ ____ _____
YWTAROAMAYO, FBXX AWR IOOJ MVROH

___: ___ __ ___ __ _LL ___ _____.
SWL: SWL BI AWR BA MXX ZBI RZWTSZRI.
```

148

```
I ____ ____ ____, ___ ___ __ ___; ___
H XCGY AYYT RVDTF, CTJ TVQ CS VOJ; RYN

____ I ___ ____ ___ R_____
XCGY H TVN UYYT NXY KHFXNYVDU

__R_____, __R ___ ___ _____ _R___.
IVKUCZYT, TVK XHU UYYJ AYFFHTF AKYCJ.
```

149

```
_ _ _ _ _ _ ,    _ _ _ _    _ _ _ _ R _ _ _    _ R _ _ _    _ _    _ _ _
NIKWJQ,    OKWT    QICESICO    OSTOK    EX    OKI

_ _ _ _ R _    _ _ R _ _ :    _ _ _    _ _    _ _ _    _ _ _ _ _ _    _ _ R _
EXBFSQ    ZFSOC:    FXQ    EX    OKI    KEQQIX    ZFSO

_ _ _ _    _ _ _ _ _    M _ _ _    M _    _ _    _ _ _ _    _ _ _ _ _ M.
OKWT    CKFJO    UFYI    UI    OW    YXWB    BECQWU.
```

150

```
C _ _ _ _ _ _ _ _ _    _ _    A _ _    _ _ _ _    _ _ A _    _ _ _ _ _
BDEZDJEFSF    AS    NKK    MISV    MINM    RSTQS

_ _ A _ _ _    _ _ A _ _ _ ,    _ _ A _    _ _ A _ _    _ _ _ _ _ _ _ _ _ _
PTNQSE    HLNPSR,    MINM    ADNRM    MISLRSKQSR

_ _    _ _ _ _ _ :    _ _ _ _ _ _ _    _ _ _ ,    A _ _    _ _    _ _ _ _ .
DZ    HFDKR:    XDTRIHG    IHL,    NKK    VS    PDFR.
```

151

```
_ _ _    _ _ _    _ _ _ _ _ _    _ _ _ _    _ _ _    _ _ _ _ ,    _ _ _    _ _
YMWX    XQE    TAJBIL    AVCL    XQI    HCJB,    MLB    QI

_ _ _ _ _    _ _ _ _ _ I _    _ _ _ _ :    _ _    _ _ _ _ _    _ _ V _ _
WQMHH    WAWXMRL    XQII:    QI    WQMHH    LIUIJ

_ _ _ _ _ _    _ _ _    _ I _ _ _ _ _ _    _ _    _ _    _ _ V _ _ .
WAKKIJ    XQI    JRPQXICAW    XC    TI    FCUIB.
```

152

```
___ ____ _____ ___ _____L _F ___
KQD CRHM UHPYZDKQ KQD ORLYEDC RS KQD

_____ __ _____:  __ _____ ___
QDGKQDY KR YRLZQK:  QD XGVDKQ KQD

__V____ _F ___ ____L_ _F ____
MDFPODE RS KQD WDRWCD RS YRYD

_FF___.
DSSDOK.
```

153

```
__E__E_ __ __E _E___E ____ ____ __E
WPDOODL ZO MGD ADYAPD MGTM BJYN MGD

J_____ _____:  __E_ _____ ____, _ ____,
CYKIEP OYEJL:  MGDK OGTPP NTPB, Y PYHL,

__ __E _____ __ ___ _____E____E.
ZJ MGD PZUGM YI MGK RYEJMDJTJRD.
```

154

```
_____ B_ MA__ __A_ _A_, ___ ____ ____
KSXQX HX ZBDJ KSBK YBJ, GSC GTAA YSXG

__ A__ ____?  ____, ____ ____ __ ___
FY BDJ WCCR?  ACQR, ATUK KSCF FI KSX

_____ __ ___ _____A___ ____ __.
ATWSK CU KSJ LCFDKXDBDLX FICD FY.
```

155

____ ___ _P_____ _____ _____ _____
QLZT ZUM QYENFUZ ZUMEM VENCMZU RNFUZ

__ ___ _____: __ __ _____, ___
NL ZUM SVEGLMCC: UM NC FEVONTQC, VLS

____ __ __MP_____, ___ _____.
WQRR TW OTBYVCCNTL, VLS ENFUZMTQC.

156

__M_MB__ ____, ____ ___ ___M_ ____
KMJMJEMK DPYB, DPRD DPM MLMJT PRDP

_____, _ ____, ___ ____ ___
KMSKVRZPMW, V UVKW, RLW DPRD DPM

_____ _____ ____ B_____M__ ___
CVVUYBP SMVSUM PRGM EURBSPMJMW DPT

__M_.
LRJM.

157

_____ U___ __ ___; ___ _ __ ___UG__
JDDQEN TEDM GB FXB; WMX S JG AXMTPCD

____ ___: _____ __ ____ __
YQXB KMU: NQKSYQX GQ WXMG GB

_____U____; ___ ____ ___ _____G__
LQXZQFTDMXZ; WMX DCQB JXQ ZDXMEPQX

____ _.
DCJE S.

158

__ _____ ____ ____ _ ____ __ ____
OC KVHBJ VQJS PZQQ Z QZUR WM WHRS

___ C_MM___M____, ___C_ _ ____ _____;
RKC TSOOVHBOLHRJ, PKZTK Z KVGL QSGLB;

___ _ ____ M_______ __ ___ ________.
VHB Z PZQQ OLBZRVRL ZH RKC JRVRWRLJ.

159

_O_ _ ____ ____, ____Y _____ __ _____
HXT D NSWR QSDZ, YRTIM QNSCC AR AEDCJ

__ _O_ ____: __Y ____________ _____
EF HXT RWRT: JNM HSDJNHECLRQQ QNSCJ

__O_ _________ __ ___ ___Y _______.
JNXE RQJSACDQN DL JNR WRTM NRSWRLQ.

160

_ ____ ______ ___ L_R_ _________ __
C DCEE QFWCZT SMT EGFK WUUGFKCRO SG

___ _____________: ___ ____ ____
MCZ FCOMSTGLZRTZZ: WRK DCEE ZCRO

______ __ ___ ____ __ ___ L_R_ ____
QFWCZT SG SMT RWVT GY SMT EGFK VGZS

____.
MCOM.

161

___ _____, _ _____, A__ A ___ ____ __
RPS SWFP, F AFDU, KDS K BFU CPAA FC

_____A_____, A__ __A_____,
ZFVYKJJQFG, KGU BDKZQFPJ,

_____E____, A__ __E__E___ __ _E___
AFGBJPCCODQGB, KGU YAOGSOFPJ QG VODZH

A__ _____.
KGU SDPSW.

- -

162

__ ___ ___, ___ W__ __ _____T: T__
IF TQK BQM, JLF XIS LF VZKTZWN: NJZ

W___ __ T__ ____ __ T____: __ __ _
XQKM QT NJZ DQKM LF NKLZM: JZ LF I

B_____ T_ ___ T____ T__T T___T __
ARWYDZK NQ IDD NJQFZ NJIN NKRFN LP

___.
JLC.

- -

163

_____ __, _ ___, ___ _____ _Y _____
BYIJW RW, N JNI, TEI HDWTI RF VTYAW

_____ __ _____Y _____: _ _____ __
TJTSEAU TE YEJNIDF ETUSNE: N IWDSMWO

__ F___ ___ _____F__ ___ _____
RW XONR UQW IWVWSUXYD TEI YEBYAU

___.
RTE.

164

```
G____ _O_, _ ____, ___ _____ O_ ___
RXLBS BES, E IEXU, SCZ UZWQXZW ED SCZ

_____: _U_____ _O_ ___ _____
MQTJZU: DNXSCZX BES CQW MQTJZU

_____; ____ ____ _____ ____ _____.
UZKQTZ; IZWS SCZG ZYLIS SCZPWZIKZW.

_____.
WZILC.
```

165

```
___ ____ __ _____ _N___ _____ ____
BOY IBON WI ZHLZZAWCPNX EWNNZA QWSM

___ ____N_N_ __ _____ ____ ___ __
SMZ ILBYCWCP BE SMBIZ SMGS GYZ GS

____, _N_ ____ ___ __N___P_ __ ___
ZGIZ, GCA QWSM SMZ LBCSZRVS BE SMZ

P____.
VYBOA.
```

166

```
_ ____ ___ __ _____D _____ _____
V OVKK RHU XT OVISHP UDVXB EHNTQH

M___ ____: _ ____ ___ ____ __ ___M
YVXH HLHR: V DGUH UDH OTQS TN UDHY

____ ____ ___D_; __ _____ ___ _____
UDGU UMQX GRVPH; VU RDGKK XTU IKHGAH

__ M_.
UT YH.
```

167

```
_ _ E  _ O R _  _ _ E _ E _ _  _ _ E  E _ E _  _ _  _ _ E
U D I  P W X Z  W O I C I U D  U D I  I B I V  W L  U D I

_ _ _ _ _ _ :  _ _ E  _ O R _  _ _ _ _ E _ _  _ _ E _  _ _ _ _  _ _ E
F P H C Z :  U D I  P W X Z  X S H V I U D  U D I Q  U D S U  S X I

_ _ _ E _  _ _ _ _ :  _ _ E  _ O R _  _ _ _ E _ _  _ _ E
F W G I Z  Z W G C :  U D I  P W X Z  P W E I U D  U D I

_ _ _ _ _ _ E _ _ _ :
X H A D U I W T V :
```

- -

168

```
T _ _  _ _ _ _ _ _ _  _ _ _  _ _ _ _ _ ,  _ _ _  _ _ _ _ _
C I H  I H U T H Q Y  U W H  C I R Q H ,  C I H  H U W C I

_ _ _ _  _ _  _ _ _ _ _ :  _ _  _ _ _  _ _ _  _ _ _ _ D  _ _ D
U B Y V  R Y  C I R Q H :  U Y  Z V W  C I H  D V W B F  U Q F

_ _ _  _ _ _ _ _ _ _  _ _ _ _ _ _ _ ,  _ _ _ _  _ _ _ _
C I H  Z O B Q H Y Y  C I H W H V Z ,  C I V O  I U Y C

_ _ _ _ D _ D  _ _ _ _ .
Z V O Q F H F  C I H P .
```

- -

169

```
_ _  _ _ _ _  _ _ _ _  _ _ _  _ O _ _ ,  _ _ _ _ _ _  _ _ _ ;
G W  M Y S M  Z W S C  M Y W  B I C H ,  V C S D E W  Y D P ;

_ _ _  _ _  _ _ _  _ _ _ _  O _  _ _ _ O _ ,  _ _ O _ _ _ _
S B B  G W  M Y W  E W W H  I Z  O S F I L ,  K B I C D Z G

_ _ _ ;  _ N _  _ _ _ _  _ _ _ ,  _ _ _  _ _  _ _ _  _ _ _ _
Y D P ;  S R H  Z W S C  Y D P ,  S B B  G W  M Y W  E W W H

O _  _ _ _ _ _ _ .
I Z  D E C S W B .
```

170

```
___   ____     R_W_R___   __   ____R____    __   __
FYS   PNTU   TSLOTUSU   QS   OBBNTURJI   FN   QW

R_____;   ____R____   __   ___
TRIYFSNGCJSCC;   OBBNTURJI   FN   FYS

_____   __   __   _____   ____   __
BPSOJJSCC   ND   QW   YOJUC   YOFY   YS

R_____   __.
TSBNQZSJCSU   QS.
```

171

```
_____   ___   ____   ___   _____   _____
VMJDDISE   KIJ   JDIL   JDB   JXKEXO   HXONMXC

____   __,   O   _O__:   ___   ___
QOIH   HX,   I   SIOE:   SXJ   JDB

__V___K_____   ___   ___   _____
SIGMKAFMKEKXCC   WKE   JDB   JOLJD

_____   _____V_   __.
NIKJMKLWSSB   ROXCXOGX   HX.
```

172

```
_   ___E   __E   L___,   ___   _E   ___   _____:
K   ZKRV   BLV   ZKJG,   YZZ   CV   LFW   WYFOBW:

___   __E   L___   __E_E__E__   __E   _____,
NKJ   BLV   ZKJG   EJVWVJRVBL   BLV   NYFBLNTZ,

___   __E_____   _E____E__   __E   _____
YOG   EZVOBFNTZZC   JVXYJGVBL   BLV   EJKTG

__E_.
GKVJ.
```

173

```
__  ____  __N___H,  ___,  ___N  ___N___H
XI  KWZB  BWFUYDG,  IYS,  YPYF  TSJFDYDG

___  _H_  _____  __  _H_  ____:  __
TWH  DGY  OWZHDK  WT  DGY  BWHQ:  XI

H____  _N_  __  ____H  _____H  ___  ___
GYSHD  SFQ  XI  TBYKG  OHJYDG  WZD  TWH

_H_  ____N_  ___.
DGY  BJPJFU  UWQ.
```

174

```
_Y  _____  _____  ____  ___R  __  ___
JI  LZGEP  YWMXN  NWZB  WPMF  GK  NWP

__R____,  _  ___D;  __  ___  __R____  ____
JZFKGKQ,  Z  XZFA;  GK  NWP  JZFKGKQ  VGXX

_  __R___  _Y  _R_Y_R  ____  ____,  ___
G  AGFPEN  JI  TFMIPF  BKNZ  NWPP,  MKA

____  ____  __.
VGXX  XZZR  BT.
```

175

```
___,  ___  ___  ____  __E  ____  ____  ___:
WZA,  OFI  JOG  EFHZ  HTM  XZLI  GZEL  BZI:

_E_  ___  ____  _E  ____  _____  _I_
XMH  OXX  HTOH  DM  LZEFI  ODZEH  TUK

__I_G  __E_E___  ____  _I_  ____  __G__
DLUFB  JLMCMFHC  EFHZ  TUK  HTOH  ZEBTH

__  _E  _E__E_.
HZ  DM  QMOLMI.
```

176

```
___  _S  _____  __  __  _____  __  ___
XCY  DU  XEHFBAJ    BC  PH  GHFEHY  DL  BWH

_SS_____  __  ___  S____S,  ___  __  __  ___
FUUHZPAJ   CG  BWH  UFDLBU,  FLY  BC  PH  WFY

__  __V_____  __  ___  ____  ____  ___
DL  EHSHEHLRH   CG  FAA  BWHZ  BWFB  FEH

_____  ___.
FPCOB  WDZ.
```

177

```
_____  _____  A__  _____  __A__
TDZYVQ  HFFMCYTT   NCM  LYZXQ  TKNVV

_____  __  A__  ___  _A__  __  __  ____:
EFVVFU  LY  NVV  IKY  MNQT  FE  LQ  VGEY:

A__  I  ____  _____  __  ___  _____  __  ___
NCM  G  UGVV  MUYVV  GC  IKY  KFDTY  FE  IKY

L___  ___  ____.
VFZM  EFZ  YWYZ.
```

178

```
T__  ____  __  __  ___  ____  _____,  ___
FRY  SHLN  TD  TX  RTD  RHSQ  FYGMSY,  FRY

____'_  _____  __  __  _____:  ___  ____
SHLN'D  FRLHXY  TD  TX  RYKAYX:  RTD  YQYD

B_____,  ___  _____  ___,  ___  _____
ZYRHSN,  RTD  YQYSTND  FLQ,  FRY  IRTSNLYX

__  ___.
HV  GYX.
```

179

```
___   _   __   ___R   ___   _EE__;   _E_   __E   __R_
WZY   F   EL   VUUJ   EKC   KTTCD;   DTY   YMT   HUJC

_____E__   ____   _E:   ____   _R_   __   _E__
YMFKBTYM   ZVUK   LT:   YMUZ   EJY   LD   MTHV

___   __   _E___ERER;   ___E   __   __RR____,   _
EKC   LD   CTHFRTJTJ;   LEBT   KU   YEJJDFKI,   U

__   ___.
LD   IUC.
```

180

```
__   ___   D__   __   __   _____   _   _____   ___
KL   FYB   IQM   JZ   NM   FEJOXTB   K   DJOHYF   FYB

___D:   __   ____   ___   __   ___   _____,   __D
TJEI:   NM   DJEB   EQL   KL   FYB   LKHYF,   QLI

C____D   ___:   __   ____   _____D   __   __
ABQDBI   LJF:   NM   DJOT   EBZODBI   FJ   XB

C_____D.
AJNZJEFBI.
```

181

```
____   ____,   _   ___,   __   __   ___   ____K_,
HADJ   DGNN,   J   VJW,   WJ   RN   VBTN   DGPAXY,

U___   ____   __   __   ____   ____K_:   ___   ____
HADJ   DGNN   WJ   RN   VBTN   DGPAXY:   ZJF   DGPD

___   ____   __   ____   ___   ___   __U_   ___K_
DGO   APLN   BY   ANPF   DGO   RJAWFJHY   RJFXY

_____.
WNKIPFN.
```

182

```
__E__ __E ____, _E ___ ___E__, ____
EQJFF RXJ QUMG, KJ XNF VZPJQF, RXVR

E_CE_ __ ___E____, ____ __ ___
JWHJQ NZ FRMJZPRX, RXVR GU XNF

C_MM___ME___, _E___E____ ____ __E
HUIIVZGIJZRF, XJVMSJZNZP DZRU RXJ

___CE __ ___ ____.
BUNHJ UO XNF TUMG.
```

183

```
_ ____ S___ _ ___ S___ ____ ____, _
S OSYY GSVW N VDO GBVW TVLB LFDD, B

___: ____ _ _S_____ ___ __
WBR: TXBV N XGNYLDPK NVR NV

__S_____ _F ___ S_____S ____ _ S___ _
SVGLPTZDVL BE LDV GLPSVWG OSYY S GSVW

____S_S ____ ____.
XPNSGDG TVLB LFDD.
```

184

```
____ ___ ___ __ ___ ____ __LL _
NUWE KVX XTY WN KVX XJUKV DRQQ R

___ ____ ____, ____ __ ____ __
MUB FTKW KVXX, DVXT EB VXJUK RA

_____L___: L___ __ __ ___ ___K
WPXUDVXQEXY: QXJY EX KW KVX UWMO

____ __ _____ ____ _.
KVJK RA VRHVXU KVJT R.
```

185

`___ _____ _S ___ _____SS,`
JQP SGXSFFSDN ZR NJH FQOZDILZDMDSRR,

`_ ___! ___R___R_ ___ _____R__ __ ___`
Q IQM! NJSVSEQVS NJS XJZFMVSD QE CSD

`P__ ____R _R_S_ ____R ___ S_____ __`
AYN NJSZV NVYRN YDMSV NJS RJBMQP QE

`___ ____S.`
NJH PZDIR.

186

`____ _A__ _A__, ____, A__ __T __ __T`
AFLC FURL IUEZ, BPVL, USZ KLA JI BJA

`T___ ___ ____ _____ A _AT___; T_AT T__`
AFLV PTT THPV GLESX U SUAEPS; AFUA AFL

`_A__ __ ___A__ _A_ __ __ ____ __`
SUVL PT EIHULK VUC GL SP VPHL ES

`_____ _A___.`
HLVLVGHUSBL.

187

`___P __, _ ___ __ ___ _A__A____, ___`
XTKJ CI, A OAV AB ACL IGKUGMHAS, BAL

`___ ____ __ ___ _A__: A__ _____`
MXT OKALP AB MXP SGWT: GSV VTKHUTL

`__, A__ P____ A_A_ ___ ____, ___ ___`
CI, GSV JCLOT GFGP ACL IHSI, BAL MXP

`_A__'_ _A__.`
SGWT'I IGYT.

188

`_ _ _   _ _S   _ _ _ _ _ _   _ _ _ _ _ _ _ _ _   _ _ _   _   _ _ _ _ _ _;`
WAE BOQ JRKIE IRYNEIZB SNZ J XAXIRZ;

`_ _   _ _S   _ _ _ _ _ _   _S   _ _ _ _:   _ _ _ _ _ _ _   _ _ _`
OR BOQ WJPANE OQ GOWI: VIIUORK XJM

`_ _ _ _ _ _   _ _ _   _   _ _ _ _ _,   _ _ _   _ _ _   C_ _ _ _ _   _ _`
IRYNEI WAE J ROKBZ, SNZ TAM LAXIZB OR

`_ _ _   _ _ _ _ _ _ _.`
ZBI XAERORK.

- -

189

`_ _O_   _ _ _ _   _ _ _ _   _ _   _ _ _   _ _ _ _   O_   _ _ _ _:`
WBIF DOMW JBVD HV WBV QGWB IE MOEV:

`_ _   _ _Y   _ _ _ _ _ _ _ _   _ _   _ _ _ _ _ _ _   O_   _OY;   _ _`
OT WBC QAVJVTNV OJ EFMTVJJ IE ZIC; GW

`_ _Y   _ _ _ _ _   _ _ _ _   _ _ _ _ _   _ _ _   _ _ _ _ _ _ _ _`
WBC AOUBW BGTX WBVAV GAV QMVGJFAVJ

`_O_   _ _ _ _ _O_ _.`
EIA VRVAHIAV.

- -

190

`_ _ _   _ _ _ _ _ _ _ _   _ _   G_ _   _ _ _   _ _ _ _ _ _`
BEX PEFZQUBI UC OUJ FZX BGXDBS

`_ _ _U_ _ _ _,   _ _ _ _   _ _ _U_ _ _ _ _   _ _   _ _ _ _ _ _:`
BEUKIFDJ, XYXD BEUKIFDJI UC FDOXMI:

`_ _ _   _ _ _ _   _ _   _ _ _ _ _   _ _ _ _,   _ _   _ _   _ _ _ _ _,`
BEX MUZJ QI FWUDO BEXW, FI QD IQDFQ,

`_ _   _ _ _   _ _ _ _   _ _ _ _ _.`
QD BEX EUMS TMFPX.

191

`__  ____   __V_   ___   _ ___,  ____   _V__:  __`
EN BCYB XWJN BCN XWZS, CYBN NJKX: CN

`_____V___   ___   _____   __   ___   ___N__;`
OZNINZJNBC BCN IWPXI WQ CKI IYKVBI;

`__   ____V_____   ____   ___   __   ___   __N_`
CN SNXKJNZNBC BCNH WPB WQ BCN CYVS

`__   ___   _____.`
WQ BCN TKFDNS.

192

`_  _OO___   O_   __   _____   ____,   ___`
G FMMSOU MY ZW XGTJA JLYU, LYU

`_____,   ___   _____   __S  _O   ___   ____`
EOJOFU, EBA AJOXO DLH YM ZLY AJLA

`_O___   __O_   __:   _____   _____   __;  _O`
DMBFU SYMD ZO: XOVBTO VLGFOU ZO; YM

`___   _____   _O_   __   SO__.`
ZLY KLXOU VMX ZW HMBF.

193

`_____,  O  _O__,  ___   __I____N   __   ____`
DHSHSAHD, F YFDC, ZLH ULGYCDHP FT HCFS

`IN   ___   ___   __   _____;   ___   __I_,`
IN GP ZLH CWR FT KHDJBWYHS; XLF BWGC,

`____   I_,  ____   I_,   ___N  __   ___`
DWBH GZ, DWBH GZ, HNHP ZF ZLH

`___N___I_N   _____.`
TFJPCWZGFP ZLHDHFT.

194

```
_ ____   PR_____ ____; __ R _ __
A FAVV LWYANU ZBUU; IMW A YC

___R_____ ___ _____R_____ ____:
IUYWIQVVJ YRG FMRGUWIQVVJ CYGU:

__R_____ _R_ ___ __R__; ___ ____
CYWOUVVMQN YWU ZBJ FMWTN; YRG ZBYZ

__ ____ _____ R____ ____.
CJ NMQV TRMFUZB WAPBZ FUVV.
```

195

```
___ ____ _____T_ T__ _T_____; __
BOI CFSG JSIRISNIBO BOI RBSLEKISR; OI

_____T_ T__ __T_____ ___ ___O_:
SICVINIBO BOI TLBOISCIRR LEG XVGFX:

B_T T__ ___ O_ T__ _____ __ T____T_
PHB BOI XLM FT BOI XVUYIG OI BHSEIBO

_____ _O__.
HJRVGI GFXE.
```

196

```
_E B_____ _E __ ____ ___ __ __
IL RQXDWIS OL DH EFMX XDS XK EC

_____B_E ___, ___ __ __E ____ ____, ___
IXQQJRFL HJS, XDS XK SIL OJQT BFET, ECP

_E_ __ _EE_ ____ _ ____, ___
MLS OT KLLS DHXC E QXBV, ECP

E___B___E_ __ _____ _.
LMSERFJMILP OT WXJCWM.
```

197

`___ ___ _O___ O_ __ _O___, ___ ___`
MJI IDJ SEPFX EU GC GETID, ROF IDJ

`_____O_ O_ __ _____, __ _____ _L_`
GJFNIRINEO EU GC DJRPI, WJ RBBJLIRWMJ

`__ ___ _____, _ ____, __ _____, ___`
NO IDC XNYDI, E MEPF, GC XIPJOYID, ROF

`__ _____.`
GC PJFJJGJP.

198

`___ _____ S____ S__ __, ___ __`
KDF MUESFR LDPOO LFF UK, PGR QF

`_____; __ S____ ___S_ ____ __S`
ZCUFHFR; DF LDPOO ZGPLD MUKD DUL

`_____, ___ ____ ____: ___ __S___ O_`
KFFKD, PGR TFOK PMPX: KDF RFLUCF WA

`___ _____ S____ ____S_.`
KDF MUESFR LDPOO VFCULD.

199

`__ ___ ___ _____D____ __ ___ _____D`
BJ DLA AJL FOUNLHMLQQ BR AJL FOUNLH

`__M_ __ __ __D; ___ _____ ___`
UBXL AB PM LMH; ZTA LQAPZDOQJ AJL

`____: ___ ___ _____ __D _____ ___`
KTQA: RBV AJL VOEJALBTQ EBH AVOLAJ AJL

`_____ __D _____.`
JLPVAQ PMH VLOMQ.

200

```
___  ____  _  __A_  ___  ____  _A____  ___
JNE  WJNE  T  FGZF  FGD  XNHQ  VZLDFG  GTV

A_____;  __  ____  __A_  ___  ____  ___
ZJNTJFDQ;  GD  ETXX  GDZH  GTR  OHNR  GTV

____  __A___  ____  ___  _A___G  _____G__
GNXP  GDZLDJ  ETFG  FGD  VZLTJK  VFHDJKFG

__  ___  __G__  _A__.
NO  GTV  HTKGF  GZJQ.
```

- -

201

```
___  _O_  ___M  ____  ___  M___  ___M___
CAJ  PYJ  JRAL  JRQJ  QOA  LEPA  APALEAH

__O_____  __O___  O___  M_:  _____
IOYPFDMCCG  OAWYEXA  YSAO  LA:  PAEJRAO

___  ___M  ____  ____  ___  ___  ____  ____
CAJ  JRAL  IEPZ  IEJR  JRA  AGA  JRQJ  RQJA

M_  ____O__  _  _____.
LA  IEJRYMJ  Q  XQMHA.
```

- -

202

```
___  _____  ___  _____RY  __
QNY  RXBBXBD  BDX  RNFHBKGM  HV

_____:  __  _R_____  ___  _____
SKIHFHXR:  DX  CGHVQXBD  NJB  BDNRX

_____  _R_  _____  ____  _____:  ___  ___
EDHOD  KGX  CNJVY  EHBD  ODKHVR:  CJB  BDX

R_____  _____  __  _  _RY  ____.
GXCXFFHNJR  YEXFF  HV  K  YGM  FKVY.
```

203

`_I__ ___ ___ _A__ ____ __ I_ ___ _A_`
CFUQ RNK KCP DZBQ DMNL LQ FR KCQ UZP

`____ _ A_ I_ _____; I___I__ __I__`
ACQR F ZL FR KMNJTYQ; FRBYFRQ KCFRQ

`_A_ ____ __: I_ ___ _A_ ____ _ _A__`
QZM JRKN LQ: FR KCQ UZP ACQR F BZYY

`A_____ __ _____I__.`
ZRHAQM LQ HEQQUFYP.

204

`_____ ___ ___ ___ __ __ _____,`
QNVNVLNQ HDK KCN RWHR DG VA ADYKC,

`___ __ __A_____ ___: A____D___ __`
HDQ VA KQZHRFQNRRWDHR: ZEEDQSWHF KD

`___ _____ _____ ____ __ ___ ___`
KCA VNQEA QNVNVLNQ KCDY VN GDQ KCA

`___D____' _A__, _ ____.`
FDDSHNRR' RZXN, D ODQS.

205

`___ ___ __A__ __M_, A__ __A__ ___`
QAU VQK MPDXX OQBG, DZK MPDXX ZQC

`____ _____: A ____ __A__ _____`
LGGT MJXGZOG: D EJUG MPDXX KGRQAU

`_____ __M, A__ __ __A__ __ ____`
YGEQUG PJB, DZK JC MPDXX YG RGUF

`__M_____ _____ A____ __M.`
CGBTGMCAQAM UQAZK DYQAC PJB.

206

```
____ __ __A_ ___ L___ __ __ ___: __
IYGT BA RDER RDA QGJZ DA HV PGZ: HR

__ __ __A_ _A__ _A__ __, A__ ___ __
HV DA RDER DERD KEZA MV, EYZ YGR TA

_____; __ A__ ___ _____, A__ ___
GMJVAQUAV; TA EJA DHV CAGCQA, EYZ RDA

_____ __ ___ _A_____.
VDAAC GL DHV CEVRMJA.
```

- -

207

```
____ ___ _____D _____ __ ___ _____,
BYVP JYV BSZRVC NODSPL UN JYV LDUNN,

__D ____ ___ ___ _____ _F _____
UPC BYVP UKK JYV BQDRVDN QE SPSGFSJX

D_ F_____; __ __ ____ ____ _____ __
CQ EKQFDSNY; SJ SN JYUJ JYVX NYUKK WV

D_____D F__ ____:
CVNJDQXVC EQD VIVD:
```

- -

208

```
___ ___M __ ___M__ ___ _____
MLV VKLC RL EGKECLP EDP WBDOBJDPLP

____ ____ _____ M_ ____: ___ ___M __
VKEV GLLX EOVLA CZ GBJM: MLV VKLC RL

_____ _____, ___ ___ __ _____I __,
VJADLP REWXIEAP, EDP SJV VB WBDOJGHBD,

____ ___I__ M_ ____.
VKEV PLGHAL CZ KJAV.
```

209

```
_ ____ ____ ___ ___D _ ___ ____; ___
I UHRD FROI OXQ BIVS N RQG UIRD; AIV

__ ____ ____ _____LL___ _____: ___
XQ XNOX SIRQ JNVEQBBIFU OXHRDU: XHU

_____ ____, ___ ___ __L_ ___, ____
VHDXO XNRS, NRS XHU XIBK NVJ, XNOX

_____ ___ ___ _____.
DIOOQR XHJ OXQ EHPOIVK.
```

- -

210

```
__E_ _E _ ___E_ ___ ____; ____ __E_
PMXT BX I KNGXR ENF LNNQ; KMIK KMXC

_____ ___E _E ___ _EE __, ___ _E
TMWJM MIKX BX BIC PXX WK, IRQ UX

_____E_: _E____E ____, ____, ____
IPMIBXQ: UXJIDPX KMND, ANFQ, MIPK

__LPE_ _E, ___ _____E_ _E.
MNAYXR BX, IRQ JNBENFKXQ BX.
```

- -

211

```
____ _Y_S S_____ __ ____ ___ _____
FLRO ODOW WAEXX KO STQR ZAO JELZAJSX

__ ___ ____, ____ ___Y __Y _____ ____
QJ ZAO XERG, ZAEZ ZAOD FED GMOXX MLZA

__: __ ____ _____ __ _ _____ __Y,
FO: AO ZAEZ MEXIOZA LR E TOVJOBZ MED,

__ S____ S____ __.
AO WAEXX WOVPO FO.
```

212

```
__   ____   _____   ___   ___C_   ___   ___
YQ   YJHY  DQLQLUQDQK    YRB   LQDEX   JPK   YRB

_____   _____   ___   _____   __   _____:   ___
HDSHY   HZGJDK   HYQ   YZSBQ   ZN   RBDJQV:   JVV

___   ____   __   ___   _____   __V_   ____   ___
HYQ   QPKB   ZN   HYQ   QJDHY   YJCQ   BQQP   HYQ

___V_____   __   ___   ___.
BJVCJHRZP   ZN   ZSD   IZK.
```

- -

213

```
___   ____   ___,   H__   _____   ___   ____
FJS   QTMY   UYN,   OYK   MLAAXZHL   JAM   MOYQ

__   ___   ____S!   _____   ___   _____SS
XT   MOS   KYADF!   MOAYQUO   MOL   UALJMTLFF

__   ___   _____   S____   _____   _____S
YW   MOS   GYKLA   FOJHH   MOXTL   LTLEXLF

S_____   ____S____S   ____   ____.
FQZEXM   MOLEFLHPLF   QTMY   MOLL.
```

- -

214

```
___   ___   L___   L_____   _____N_,   _N_
YQM   RSC   VQMK   VQXCRS   LTKFGCAR,   UAK

_____   N__   ___   ___N__;   ____   ___
YQMEUBCRS   AQR   SDE   EUDARE;   RSCJ   UMC

_   _____   ___   ____:   ___   ___   ____   __
WMCECMXCK   YQM   CXCM:   ZTR   RSC   ECCK   QY

___   _____   ___LL   __   ___   ___.
RSC   ODPBCK   ESUVV   ZC   PTR   QYY.
```

215

```
___ ____  B_ _____ ___ ___ __
KZC CTZS MZ HNBQNABLZL PBL WAC CN

_____ ____ ___K _____ __ ____: ___ ____
FTPSZ CTPC FZZY PQCZI SD FNAK: KZC CTZS

B_ _____ B__K ___ B_____ __
MZ CAIBZL MPHY PBL MINAETC CN

_____ ____ _____ __ ____.
HNBQAFXNB CTPC LZGXFZ SD TAIC.
```

- -

216

```
_____ ___ __ ___ _____ ___ ___I T_,
TQWLKC VLZ UO KUI NLJWLL MWL YMZBHC,

___ ___ __ _I__ _____ ___ _ _I_: T_
MZN VLZ UO GBJG NLJWLL MWL M KBL: HU

__ __I_ I_ T__ _____, T___ ___
PL KMBN BZ HGL PMKMZDL, HGLC MWL

__T___T___ _I__T__ T___ ___IT_.
MKHUJLHGLW KBJGHLW HGMZ YMZBHC.
```

- -

217

```
___ __ __A__ __I__ ____ ____ ___I_
ZBS GO QGZVV RIYBP FHKB EGON EGOYI

_W_ I_I__I__, A__ __A__ ___ ____ ___
KCB YBYUFYEX, ZBS QGZVV DFE EGON KMM

I_ ___I_ _W_ WI_____; __A, ___
YB EGOYI KCB CYDLOSBOQQ; XOZ, EGO

____ ___ ___ __A__ ___ ____ __.
VKIS KFI PKS QGZVV DFE EGON KMM.
```

218

```
_  ____  _EA_  __A_  ___  __E  L___  ____
Q  SQDD  CWMY  SCMH  OUX  HCW  DUYX  SQDD

__EA_:  ___  _E  ____  __EA_  _EA_E
TGWMB:  ZUY  CW  SQDD  TGWMB  GWMRW

____  ___  _E___E,  A__  __  ___  _A____:
FVHU  CQT  GWUGDW,  MVX  HU  CQT  TMQVHT:

___  _E_  __E_  ___  ____  A_A__  __
NFH  DWH  HCWP  VUH  HFYV  MOMQV  HU

_____.
ZUDDJ.
```

219

```
____  ____  __R___  __R  __  __  ___R____
KAGC  AHUK  KCDBFN  JGD  LF  LE  LGCDBMBI

____  ___C___:  ____  ____  ___  ___  __
MBKG  NHBRMBI:  KAGC  AHUK  VCK  GJJ  LE

__C_C____,  ___  __R___  __  ____
UHRSRTGKA,  HBN  IMDNFN  LF  XMKA

_____;  __  ___  ___  ____  __  ___R_
ITHNBFUU;  KG  KAF  FBN  KAHK  LE  ITGDE

___  ____  _R____  __  ____,  ___  ___  __
LHE  UMBI  VDHMUF  KG  KAFF,  HBN  BGK  QF

_____.  _  ___D  __  ___,  _  ____  ____
UMTFBK.  G  TGDN  LE  IGN,  M  XMTT  IMOF

_____  ____  ____  __R  ___R.
KAHBSU  CBKG  KAFF  JGD  FOFD.
```

220

```
_HE  _E__  __  _HE  L___  __  _HE
MPT  BTYL  IB  MPT  UILG  AR  MPT

_E_____  __  _____:  _  ____
WTVASSASV    IB  JARGIE:   Y  VIIG

___E_____  H__E  ___  _HE_  _H__  __
XSGTLRMYSGASV   PYOT  YUU  MPTZ  MPYM  GI

H__  _____E___:  H__  _____E  E____E_H
PAR  KIEEYSGETSMR:   PAR  QLYART  TSGXLTMP

___  E_E_.
BIL  TOTL.
```

221

```
G___  __  ___  ____,  ___  _____Y  __  __
EAQWO DP  OIQ VJAR,   WCR EAQWOVT  OJ  NQ

_____  __  ___  ___Y  __  ___  G__,  __
SAWDPQR  DC  OIQ YDOT  JM  JLA EJR,  DC

___  _____  __  ___  _____.
OIQ  XJLCOWDC JM  IDP IJVDCQPP.

_____  ___  _____,  ___  J_Y  __
NQWLODMLV  MJA PDOLWODJC,   OIQ FJT  JM

___  _____  _____,  __  _____  ____,  __  ___
OIQ HIJVQ  QWAOI,  DP  XJLCO  ZDJC,  JC  OIQ

_____  __  ___  _____,  ___  ___Y  __  ___
PDRQP  JM OIQ CJAOI,   OIQ YDOT  JM  OIQ

_____  ____.
EAQWO GDCE.
```

222

```
_ _  C_ _ _ _ _ _H  _H_  _ _ _ _ _ _ _  _ _  _ _C_ _ _
OM   RIYJMAO   AOM  TIEWYLJ  AW   IJRMVC

_ _ _ _  _H_  _ _ _ _  _ _  _H_  _ _ _ _H;  H_
ZLWB  AOM  MVCJ  WZ  AOM  MILAO;  OM

_ _ _ _ _ _H  _ _ _H_ _ _ _ _ _  _ _ _  _H_  _ _ _ _;  H_
BIHMAO  SGKOAVGVKJ  ZWL  AOM  LIGV;  OM

_ _ _ _ _ _ _H  _H_  _ _ _ _  _ _ _  _ _  H_ _
PLGVKMAO  AOM  QGVC  WYA  WZ  OGJ

_ _ _ _ _ _ _ _ _ _ _.
ALMIJYLGMJ.
```

- -

223

```
_ _ _ _,  _  _ _ _ _  _ _  _O_,  _ _ _  _ _ _  _O_ _ _ _ _ _ _
NBLS,  G  XGPC  NS  IGC,  BPD  FJS  AGLCDPRWX

_O_ _ _  _ _ _C_  _ _O_  _ _ _ _  _O_ _,  _ _ _  _ _ _
AGPVY  AJUOJ  FJGW  JBYF  CGLD,  BLC  FJS

_ _O_ G_ _ _  _ _ _C_  _ _ _  _O  _ _-_ _ _ _:  _ _ _ _
FJGWIJFY  AJUOJ  BPD  FG  WY-ABPC:  FJDS

C_ _ _O_  _ _  _ _C_O_ _ _  _ _  _ _  O_ _ _ _  _ _ _O
OBLLGF  HD  PDOVGLDC  WQ  UL  GPCDP  WLFG

_ _ _ _:  _ _  _  _O_ _ _  _ _C_ _ _ _  _ _ _  _ _ _ _ _  O_
FJDD:  UR  U  AGWXC  CDOXBPD  BLC  YQDBV  GR

_ _ _ _,  _ _ _ _  _ _ _  _O_ _  _ _ _ _  C_ _  _ _
FJDN,  FJDS  BPD  NGPD  FJBL  OBL  HD

_ _ _ _ _ _ _ _.
LWNHDPDC.
```

224

```
___,    _H_Y  _____    _H_  _____
AYG,    QWYA  KYXOLXYK    QWY  ONYGXGHQ

_____,    _H_Y  _____    ___    H__  W___:___
NGHK,    QWYA  MYNLYFYK    HTQ    WLX  DTSK:MEQ

_____  __  _H___  _____,  ___
PESPESYK  LH  QWYLS  QYHQX,  GHK

H_____  ___  ____  _H_  _____  __  _H_
WYGSIYHYK  HTQ  EHQT  QWY  FTLVY  TZ  QWY

____.
NTSK.
```

225

```
___  _N__  ___  _____  G__  _____,  ____
MSP  SJPR  PNI  DELAIO  KRO  WUEPN,  DNUP

____  ____  __  __  __  _____  __
NUWP  PNRS  PR  OR  PR  OILCUVI  QF

_____,  __  ____  ____  _____
WPUPSPIW,  RV  PNUP  PNRS  WNRSCOIWP

____  __  ____N_N_  _N  ___  _____?  ____N_
PUAI  QF  LRZIJUJP  EJ  PNF  QRSPN?  WIIEJK

____  _____  _N_____N,  _N_  _____
PNRS  NUPIWP  EJWPVSLPERJ,  UJO  LUWPIWP

__  _____  ____N_  ____.
QF  DRVOW  MINEJO  PNII.
```

226

```
_ _ _,   _H_ _ _H   _   _ _ _ _   _H_ _ _ _H   _H_
WGQ,  BIPTKI  H  VQFA  BIDPTKI  BIG

_ _ _ _ _Y   _ _   _H_   _H_ _ _   _ _   _ _ _ _H,   _   _ _ _ _
ZQFFGW  PN  BIG  YIQCPV  PN  CGQBI,  H  VHFF

_ _ _ _   _ _   _ _ _ _:   _ _ _   _H_ _   _ _ _   _ _ _H   _ _;
NGQD  SP  GZHF:  NPD  BIPT  QDB  VHBI  OG;

_HY   _ _ _   _ _ _   _HY   _ _ _ _ _   _H_Y   _ _ _ _ _ _ _
BIW  DPC  QSC  BIW  YBQNN  BIGW  EPONPDB

_ _.
OG.
```

- -

227

```
_ _ _   _ _ _ _ _   _AV_   _   _ _ _ _ _ _ _   O_   _ _ _
YZM  DAPZJ  AWIM  P  CMBPLMC  YE  DAM

_ _ _ _,   _ _A_   _ _ _ _   _   _ _ _ _   A_ _ _ _;   _ _A_   _
XYLC,  DAWD  OPXX  P  BMMN  WEDML;  DAWD  P

_A_   _ _ _ _ _   _ _   _ _ _   _O_ _ _   O_   _ _ _   _ _ _ _
HWS  COMXX  PZ  DAM  AYQBM  YE  DAM  XYLC

A_ _   _ _ _   _A_ _   O_   _ _   _ _ _ _,   _O   _ _ _O_ _
WXX  DAM  CWSB  YE  HS  XPEM,  DY  GMAYXC

_ _ _   _ _A_ _ _   O_   _ _ _   _ _ _ _,   A_ _   _O
DAM  GMWQDS  YE  DAM  XYLC,  WZC  DY

_ _ _ _ _ _ _   _ _   _ _ _   _ _ _ _ _ _.
MZVQPLM  PZ  APB  DMHTXM.
```

228

_ _ _ _ _ _   T _ _   _ _ _ N T _ _ N _   _ _ _ _   _ _ _ _ _ _ T
LVPUMV SBV KUTRSYFRN JVMV LMUTCBS

_ _ _ T _,   _ _   _ _ _ _   T _ _ _   _ _ _ _ T   _ _ _ _ _ _   T _ _
PUMSB, UM VZVM SBUT BYHNS PUMKVH SBV

_ _ _ T _   _ N _   T _ _   _ _ _ _ _,   _ _ _ N   _ _ _ _
VYMSB YRH SBV JUMXH, VZVR PMUK

_ _ _ _ _ _ _ T _ N _   T _   _ _ _ _ _ _ _ T _ N _,   T _ _ _   _ _ T
VZVMXYNSFRC SU VZVMXYNSFRC, SBUT YMS

_ _ _.
CUH.

- -

229

_ _ _ T   _ _ _   _ _   _ _   T _ _ T   _ _ _ _ _ _ T _   _ _ _ _,
ZUPD RPG CL UX DUPD NXLCVXDU MCKX,

_ _ _   _ _ _ _ T _   _ _ _ _   _ _ _ _,   T _ _ T   _ _   _ _ _   _ _ _
PGN MFEXDU RPGO NPOL, DUPD UX RPO LXX

_ _ _ _?   _ _ _ _   T _ _   T _ _ _ _ _   _ _ _ _   _ _ _ _,   _ _ _
HFFN? JXXS DUO DFGHTX KVFR XECM, PGN

T _ _   _ _ _ _   _ _ _ _   _ _ _ _ _ _ _ _   _ _ _ _ _.   _ _ _ _ _ T
DUO MCSL KVFR LSXPJCGH HTCMX. NXSPVD

_ _ _ _   _ _ _ _,   _ _ _   _ _   _ _ _ _;   _ _ _ _   _ _ _ C _,
KVFR XECM, PGN NF HFFN; LXXJ SXPAX,

_ _ _   _ _ _ _ _ _   _ T.
PGN STVLTX CD.

230

____ ___ ___ _____ __ ___ ____
SXQA TRH NLV BNLSX PZWWQG TZSX

_ __G____, ___ ___ ___G__ ____
WRLFXSQV, RAG NLV SNAFLQ TZSX

___G__G: ____ ____ ____ ____G ___
HZAFZAF: SXQA HRZG SXQC RBNAF SXQ

_____, ___ ___D ____ ____ G____
XQRSXQA, SXQ WNVG XRSX GNAQ FVQRS

_____G_ ___ ____.
SXZAFH PNV SXQB.

- -

231

_____ __ ___ ___ W___ ____
CHUXXUE NX POU IZF VOMI POMT

___ _____, ___ _____ __ _____
BOMMXUXP, ZFE BZTXUXP PM ZSSAMZBO

____ ____, ____ __ ___ _W___ __ ___
TFPM POUU, POZP OU IZW EVUHH NF POW

_____: W_ _____ __ _____ W___
BMTAPX: VU XOZHH CU XZPNXYNUE VNPO

___ _____ __ ___ _____, _V__ __
POU QMMEFUXX MY POW OMTXU, ULUF MY

___ ____ _____.
POW OMHW PUISHU.

232

```
_ __   _   ___   __      T__   C___T_   __   __TT__
WNV    H   SHQ   BA      KTQ   RNJVKI   BI   UCKKCV

T___   _   T_____.   _   ___   __T___   __   _
KTHA   H   KTNJIHAS.    B   THS   VHKTCV   UC   H

_____   __         T__   _____   __   __   ___,
SNNVMCCGCV   BA         KTC   TNJIC   NW   LQ   ONS,

T___   T_   _____   __   T__   T__T_   __
KTHA   KN   SYCZZ   BA   KTC   KCAKI   NW

__C_____.
YBRMCSACII.
```

233

```
___   ____   _____   ___   ___,   ___   __   _L__,
EXZ   ZMXK   OMNVZ   HNG   BNC,   QSW   IX   AEQW,

____   _____   __   _I_____   _____:   ___,
ZMQZ   HQLNVG   KC   GFAMZXNVO   YQVOX:   CXQ,

L__   ____   ___   ____I___LL_,   ___   ___
EXZ   ZMXK   OQC   YNSZFSVQEEC,    EXZ   ZMX

___D   __   ____I_I__,   __I__   ____
ENGW   IX   KQASFHFXW,   DMFYM   MQZM

_L_____   I_   ___   _____I__   __   _I_
UEXQOVGX   FS   ZMX   UGNOUXGFZC   NH   MFO

_____.
OXGLQSZ.
```

234

```
___ ___ ____ __S_ ____, _ __ S___? ___
POQ SJV VOAD NSUV YAPB, A IQ UADX? SBY

___ ___ ____ __S_____ __ __? ____
POQ SJV VOAD YFUCDFMVMY FB IM? OARM

____ __ G__: ___ _ S____ ___ ____S_
VOAD FB WAY: TAJ F UOSXX QMV RJSFUM

___ ___ ___ ____ __ __S _____.
OFI TAJ VOM OMXR AT OFU NADBVMBSBNM.
```

235

```
_H__ V_____ _H_ ___ _H, ___
WCPE YGRGWBRW WCB BUMWC, UZI

_____ __: _H__ _____
OUWBMBRW GW: WCPE XMBUWKT

___ __H___ __ ___H _H_ __V__ __ ___,
BZMGSCBRW GW OGWC WCB MGYBM PD XPI,

_H__H __ ____ __ _____: _H__
OCGSC GR DEKK PD OUWBM: WCPE

_____ _H__ ____, _H__ _H__ H___
QMBQUMBRW WCBV SPMZ, OCBZ WCPE CURW

__ ___V____ ___ __.
RP QMPYGIBI DPM GW.
```

236

```
__Y _MO__ ___ _____ ____ ___ ____
FVN VIHDL BUS USVBUSD BUVB BUS KHGO

_____: ___ _O___ ___O _____ __
GSWLDSBU: BUS XHGKO VKFH FUVKK RS

_____ ____ __ _____ _O_ __
SFBVRKWFUSO BUVB WB FUVKK DHB RS

MO___: __ _____ _____ ___ __O___
IHESO: US FUVKK YMOLS BUS QSHQKS

_____O___Y.
GWLUBSHMFKN.
```

- -

237

```
__ _____ ___O __, _ _O_, __ _____
TL QLSZFEXP XMVI QL, I NIK, TL QLSZFEXP

___O __: _O_ __ SO__ ___S____ __ ____:
XMVI QL: EIS QB DIXP VSXDVLVY FM VYLL:

___, __ ___ S___O_ O_ ___ ____S ____
BLR, FM VYL DYRKIH IE VYB HFMND HFPP

_ ____ __ _____, _____ ___S_
F QRJL QB SLEXNL, XMVFP VYLDL

_____S __ O__P_S_.
ZRPRQFVFLD TL IWLSORDV.
```

238

```
___  _  ____    S___   __   ___   ____R;  ___,  _
CLD  X  FXKK  IXWE  HO  DJZ  UHFTQ;  ZTY,  X

____   S___   _____   __   ___   __R__   __   ___
FXKK  IXWE  YKHLR  HO  DJZ  GTQAZ  XW  DJT

__R____:  __R  ____  __S_  ____   __
GHQWXWE:  OHQ  DJHL  JYID  CTTW  GZ

_____   ___   R_____   __   ___  ___  __  __
RTOTWAT  YWR  QTOLET  XW  DJT  RYZ  HO  GZ

_R_____.
DQHLCKT.
```

- -

239

```
_____   __T_  B_____   __   ____T;  ___  _
JGEJDLYP  PLKP  VJDMGO  ST  PGLJK;  LOB  A

__  ____   __   _____:  ___  _  _____
LS  ZQWW  DZ  PGLNAOGXX:  LOB  A  WDDMGB

___  ____   T_  T___   __T_,  B_T  T____   ___
ZDJ  XDSG  KD  KLMG  EAKT,  VQK  KPGJG  ILX

____;  ___  ___  _____T___,  B_T  _  _____
ODOG;  LOB  ZDJ  YDSZDJKGJX,  VQK  A  ZDQOB

____.
ODOG.
```

240

```
___ ____ __A__ _____ ___ __A_ __
TAV GUWB BUYII MEMVK ALM GUYG WB

_____ P_A_ ____ ____ __ A ____
RACIK QVYK DLGA GUMM WL Y GWHM

____ ____ _A____ __ _____: _____
OUML GUAD HYKMBG NM TADLC: BDVMIK

__ ___ _____ __ ___A_ _A____ ____
WL GUM TIAACB AT RVMYG OYGMVB GUMK

__A__ ___ ____ ____ ____ ___.
BUYII LAG XAHM LWRU DLGA UWH.
```

- -

241

```
_ ____ _OR____ _O__R_ ___ _O__
U QUDD QTCPLUN ZTQJCY ZLH LTDH

_____, ___ _R____ ___ ____ _OR ___
ZXONDX, JWY NCJUPX ZLH WJOX RTC ZLH

_O_____ ___ _OR ___ _R___:
DTMUWBVUWYWXPP JWY RTC ZLH ZCFZL:

_OR __O_ ____ _____ ___ _OR_
RTC ZLTF LJPZ OJBWURUXY ZLH QTCY

__O__ ___ ___ ____.
JETMX JDD ZLH WJOX.
```

```
__ ____ ___ _____O_ OF _____ ____
IF OFGO OFX YGMPGOHIA IL HYCGXM SXCX

_O__ O__ OF __O_! ____ _O_ _____
DIEX IKO IL UHIA! SFXA TIJ QCHATXOF

____ ___ _____Y OF ___ __O___,
QGDR OFX DGVOHPHON IL FHY VXIVMX,

___O_ _____ __O___, ___ _____
WGDIQ YFGMM CXWIHDX, GAJ HYCGXM

_____ __ ____.
YFGMM QX TMGJ.
```

- -

```
O_ ___ _____ __ ___ _____, ___C_
MG GMP ZFTIW RD WGA ZMMSQTDD, PGRVG

____ ____ ____ __ ___ ____ ____
WGMB GIDW JIRS BX EMF WGTL WGIW

____ ____; ___C_ ____ ____ _____
ETIF WGTT; PGRVG WGMB GIDW PFMBZGW

___ ____ ____ ____ __ ____ _____
EMF WGTL WGIW WFBDW RQ WGTT OTEMFT

___ ____ __ ___!
WGT DMQD ME LTQ!
```

244

```
_ _ _ _   _ _ _   _ _ _ _ _ _ _S   _ _   _ _ _ _ _S   _ _ _ _
YWIK    YWI   BWTKKIRZ     LU   ETYINZ   EINI

S_ _ _,   _ _ _   _ _ _   _ _ _ _ _ _ _ _I_ _S   _ _   _ _ _   _ _ _ _ _
ZIIK,   TKS   YWI   ULQKSTYCLKZ        LU   YWI   ELNRS

_ _ _ _   _IS_ _ _ _ _ _ _   _ _   _ _ _   _ _ _ _ _ _,   _   _ _ _ _,
EINI   SCZBLGINIS      TY   YWM   NIOQVI,    L   RLNS,

_ _   _ _ _   _ _ _S_   _ _   _ _ _   _ _ _ _ _ _   _ _   _ _ _
TY   YWI   ORTZY   LU   YWI   ONITYW   LU   YWM

_ _S_ _I_S.
KLZYNCRZ.
```

245

```
_ _ _   L_ _ _   _S   _ _   S_ _ _ _ _ _ _   _ _ _   _ _
IVX   MUKC   JQ   YE   QIKXHAIV   RHC   YE

S_ _ _ _ _;   _ _   _ _ _ _ _   _ _ _S_ _ _   _ _   _ _ _,   _ _ _   _
QVJXMC;   YE   VXRKI   IKGQIXC   JH   VJY,   RHC   J

_ _   _ _ _ _ _ _ _:   _ _ _ _ _ _ _ _ _   _ _   _ _ _ _ _   _ _ _ _ _ _ _
RY   VXMLXC:   IVXKXPUKX   YE   VXRKI   AKXRIME

_ _J_ _ _ _ _;   _ _ _   _ _ _ _   _ _   S_ _ _   _ _ _ _   _
KXZUJOXIV;   RHC   DJIV   YE   QUHA   DJMM   J

_ _ _ _S_   _ _ _.
LKRJQX   VJY.
```

246

```
___   __E_E  __E_  ____  _____E_  __  ____
LXG   DCUGU  DCUO  DCTD  ITGGVUZ   EB  TFTO

_____E  _E____E_  __  __  _  ___G;  ___
ITJDVQU  GUHEVGUZ   XL  EB  T  BXRN;  TRZ

__E_  ____  ____E_  __  _E____E_  __  __
DCUO  DCTD  FTBDUZ  EB  GUHEVGUZ   XL  EB

_____,  _____G,  ___G  __  __E  __  __E
WVGDC,  BTOVRN,  BVRN  EB  XRU  XL  DCU

___G_   __  ____.
BXRNB   XL  MVXR.
```

247

```
_____  __  __  ___R  ___  _____
MWPEN  LN  XZ  JNWQ  XJF  BZUKGHDKGOGNEE

__  ___  __R____;  __R  __  ____  __  I
KG  XJN  LZQGKGH;   SZQ  KG  XJNN  OZ  K

_R___:  _  ____  __  __  ____  ___  ___
XQPEX:  MWPEN  LN  XZ  DGZR  XJN  RWF

___R___  I  _____  ____;  __R  I  ____  __
RJNQNKG   K  EJZPBO  RWBD;  SZQ  K  BKSX  PV

__  ____  ____  ____.
LF  EZPB  PGXZ  XJNN.
```

`__ __A_ ___ _A__A____ __ ___A__ W___`
XT ZTOZ ZTD MOPUOZEXK XL EMQODP CDQD

`____ ___ __ ____! W___ ___ ____`
FXID XJZ XL YEXK! CTDK ZTD PXQG

`_____ _A__ ___ _A_____ __ ___`
SQEKWDZT SOFA ZTD FONZEUEZH XL TEM

`_____, _A___ __A__ __J____, A__`
NDXNPD, BOFXS MTOPP QDBXEFD, OKG

`___A__ __A__ __ __A_.`
EMQODP MTOPP SD WPOG.

`____ __ _S ___ _____ __ ___ ___, _I__`
XIIR HI OP ZQI ORRTI JS ZQI IUI, QCBI

`__ _____ ___ S_____ __ ___ _I__S,`
HI NLBIY ZQI PQOBJM JS ZQU MCLWP,

`____ ___ _I____ ____ _____SS __, ____`
SYJH ZQI MCKXIB ZQOZ JRRYIPP HI, SYJH

`__ _____ ____I_S, ___ _____SS __`
HU BIOBTU ILIHCIP, MQJ KJHROPP HI

`_____.`
OAJNZ.

250

`___ _O__ __ M_ ____, ___ M_ _____,`
UTG SVAK NR YQ AVXF, BMK YQ EVAUAGRR,
`___ M_ _____; M_ G__, M_`
BMK YQ KGSNHGAGA; YQ OVK, YQ
`_____, __ ___M _ ____ _____; M_`
RUAGMOUT, NM ZTVY N ZNSS UACRU; YQ
`_____, ___ ___ ____ __ M_`
PCXFSGA, BMK UTG TVAM VE YQ
`_____, ___ M_ ____ _____.`
RBSHBUNVM, BMK YQ TNOT UVZGA.

· ·

251

`___ T__Y __T __T T__ ____ __`
YMK NJHU OMN AMN NJH GDAL VA
`_____ _Y T____ ___ ____,`
SMIIHIIVMA FU NJHVK MEA IEMKL,
`___T___ ___ T____ ___ ___ ____ T___:`
AHVNJHK LVL NJHVK MEA DKX IDZH NJHX:
`__T T_Y ____T ____, ___ T____ ___,`
FWN NJU KVOJN JDAL, DAL NJVAH DKX,
`___ T__ ____T __ T_Y ___T_____,`
DAL NJH GVOJN MY NJU QMWANHADAQH,
`_____ T___ ____T _ _____ __T_`
FHQDWIH NJMW JDLIN D YDZMWK WANM
`T___.`
NJHX.

252

```
_ _ _ _    M_,   _   _ _ _ _,   _ _ _M   _ _ _   _ _ _ _ _   _ _
TNNL   SN,  C   ZCEU,  KECS   HGN   GRQUP   CK

_ _ _   W_ _ _ _ _;   _ _ _ _ _ _ _ _   M_   _ _ _M   _ _ _
HGN   VWJTNU;   LENPNEON   SN   KECS   HGN

_ _ _ _ _ _ _   M_ _;   W_ _   _ _ _ _   _U_ _ _ _ _   _ _
OWCZNQH   SRQ;   VGC   GRON   LAELCPNU   HC

_ _ _ _ _ _ _ _ _W   M_   _ _ _ _ _ _.
CONEHGECV   SX   DCWQDP.
```

253

```
T_ _   _ _ _ _   _ _ _LL   _ _ _ _ _   _ _ _   _ _ _ _L_:
LAO   TRSG   QAYTT   PDGZO   LAO   MORMTO:

_ _ _ _ _   _ _,   _   _ _ _ _,   _ _ _ _ _ _ _ _ _   _ _   _ _
PDGZO   EO,   R   TRSG,   YXXRSGBWZ   LR   EV

_ _ _ _ _ _ _ _ _ _ _ _,   _ _ _   _ _ _ _ _ _ _ _ _   _ _   _ _ _ _
SBZALORDQWOQQ,   YWG   YXXRSGBWZ   LR   EBWO

_ _ _ _ _ _ _ _   _ _ _ _   _ _   _ _   _ _.
BWLOZSBLV   LAYL   BQ   BW   EO.
```

254

```
_ _ _ _   _ _   _ _ _   _ _ _D,   _ _ _   _ _ _ _   _ _ _   _ _ _,
NUVE   RL   EMO   BRTG,   ULG   JOOZ   MVH   NUC,

_ _ _   _ _   _ _ _LL   _ _ _L_   _ _ _ _   _ _   _ _ _ _ _ _ _
ULG   MO   HMUBB   ODUBE   EMOO   ER   VLMOTVE

_ _ _   L_ _ _:   _ _ _ _   _ _ _   _ _ _ _ _   _ _ _   _ _ _
EMO   BULG:   NMOL   EMO   NVYJOG   UTO   YSE

_ _ _,   _ _ _ _   _ _ _L_   _ _ _   _ _.
RWW,   EMRS   HMUBE   HOO   VE.
```

255

```
_ _ _ _ ,   _ Y _ _ _ _ _     I _   _ _ _   _ _ _ _ _ _ _ Y ,   _ _ _
AMTU,  JI  ZHRTK  EL  XMK  ZROPZKI,  XMT

_ I _ _   _ Y _ _   _ _ _ _ Y :   _ _ I _ _ _ _   _ _   _
JEXH  HIHL  AMWKI:  XHEKZHT  UM  E

_ _ _ _ _ _ I _ _   _ Y _ _ _ _   I _   _ _ _ _ _   _ _ _ _ _ _ _ ,   _ _
HGHTBELH  JILHAW  EX  PTHRK  JRKKHTL,  MT

I _   _ _ I _ _ _   _ _ _   _ I _ _   _ _ _   _ _ .
EX  KZEXPL  KMM  ZEPZ  WMT  JH.
```

- -

256

```
BU _   U _ _ _   _ _ _   _ _ _ _ _ _   _ _ _   _ _ _ _ _ ,   _ _ _ _
TYS  YBSQ  SLM  DAZHMW  VQW  EFASL,  DLFS

_ _ _ _   _ _ _ U   _ _   _ _   _ _   _ _ _ _ _ _ _   _ _
LFES  SLQY  SQ  WQ  SQ  WMZXFPM  UG

_ _ _ _ U _ _ _ ,   _ _   _ _ _ _   _ _ _ U   _ _ _ U _ _   _ _ _   _ _ _ _ _
ESFSYSME,  QP  SLFS  SLQY  ELQYXWMES  SFHM

_ _   _ _ _ _ _ _ _ _   _ _   _ _ _   _ _ U _ _ ?
UG  ZQNMBFBS  AB  SLG  UQYSL?
```

- -

257

```
_ _ _   F O O _   _ _ _ _   _ _ _ _   _ _   _ _ _   _ _ _ _ _ ,   _ _ _ _ _
FJD  CQQV  JIFJ  LIPG  PB  JPL  JDIHF,  FJDHD

_ _   _ O _ _ O _ .   _ _ _ _   _ _ _   _ O _ _ _ _ _ ,   _ _ _ _   _ _ _ _
PL  BQ  AQG.  FJDU  IHD  YQHHSZF,  FJDU  JIND

_ O _ _   _ _ O _ _ _ _ _   _ O _ _ _ ,   _ _ _ _ _   _ _   _ O _ _
GQBD  IRQTPBIRVD  MQHWL,  FJDHD  PL  BQBD

_ _ _ _   _ O _ _ _   _ O O _ .
FJIF  GQDFJ  AQQG.
```

258

```
_ _ _   _ _ _   K _ _ _   _ _ _ _ _   _ _ _ _ _ _ _   _ _   G _ _ ;
INO OZQ LKUW MZPGG XQFDKTQ KU WDY;

_ _ _ _ _   _ _ _   _ _ _ _   _ _ _ _ _ _ _   _ _   _ _ M
QBQXH DUQ OZPO MVQPXQOZ IH ZKA

_ _ _ _ _   _ _ _ _ _ :   _ _ _   _ _ _   M _ _ _ _   _ _   _ _ _ M
MZPGG WGDXH: INO OZQ ADNOZ DR OZQA

_ _ _ _   _ _ _ _ K   _ _ _ _   _ _ _ _ _   _ _   _ _ _ _ _ _ _ .
OZPO MSQPL GKQM MZPGG IQ MODSSQY.
```

259

```
_ _ _   W _ _ _ _   _ _   _ _ _   _ _ _ _ _   W _ _ _   _ _ _ _ _ _ _
UJD LYSOX YG JRX HYQUJ LDSD XHYYUJDS

_ _ _ _   _ _ _ _ _ _ ,   _ _ _   W _ _   W _ _   _ _   _ _ _   _ _ _ _ _ :
UJBF PQUUDS, PQU LBS LBX RF JRX JDBSU:

_ _ _   W _ _ _ _   W _ _ _   _ _ _ _ _ _   _ _ _ _   _ _ L ,   _ _ _
JRX LYSOX LDSD XYGUDS UJBF YRW, ADU

W _ _ _   _ _ _ _   _ _ _ W _   _ W _ _ _ _ .
LDSD UJDA OSBLF XLYSOX.
```

260

```
_ _ _   _ _ _ _   _ _ ,   _ _   _ _ _ _   _ _ _ _ _ ?   _ _ _ _   _ _
VBE CRTU ER, ER BGFB BGCCP? XBGP GP

_ _ _   _ _ _ _   _ _ _ C _   _ _ D   D _ _ _ _ _ _ _   _ _   D _ _ _ _
XBR BGCC VBGNB FHQ QRPGARXB XH QVRCC

_ _ ;   _ _ _ ,   _ _ _   _ _ _ _   _ _ _ _   D _ _ _ _   _ _   _ _   _ _ _
GK; ERT, XBR CHAQ VGCC QVRCC GK GX LHA

_ _ _ _ .
RORA.
```

261

```
_ _ _ _   _ _ _ _   _ _ _ _   _ _ _ _ _ _ _   D _ _ _   C _ _ _ _ C _
BQDU  XQJI  BAXQ  YDNIWDK  RJKX  TJYYDTX

_ _ _   _ _ _   _ _ _ _ _ _ _ _ _ ,   _ _ _ _   _ _ _ _ _ _   _ _ _
FGU  EJY  AUAPIAXV,  XQJI  FGWDKX  QAK

_ _ _ _ _ _   _ _   C _ _ _ _ _ _   _ _ _ _   _ _ _ _   _   _ _ _ _ _ :
NDGIXV  XJ  TJUKIFD  GBGV  ZAWD  G  FJXQ:

_ _ _ _ _ _   _ _ _ _ _   _ _ _   _ _   _ _ _ _ _ _ _ .   _ _ _ _ _ .
KIYDZV  DCDYV  FGU  AK  CGUAXV.  KDZGQ.
```

262

```
_ _ _ _ _ R _ _ N _   _ _   _ _ _   N _ _ _ ,   _   _ _ _ ,   _ _   _ _
TXXNCFVOE  ZN  ZKD  OTLP,  N  ENF,  RN  VR

_ _ _   _ R _ _ _ _   _ N _ _   _ _ _   _ N _ _   _ _   _ _ _   _ _ R _ _ :
ZKD  BCTVRP  YOZN  ZKP  POFR  NU  ZKP  PTCZK:

_ _ _   R _ _ _ _   _ _ N _   _ _   _ _ _ _   _ _
ZKD  CVEKZ  KTOF  VR  UYQQ  NU

R _ _ _ _ _ _ _ _ N _ _ _ .
CVEKZPNYROPRR.
```

263

```
_ _   _ _ _ _ _ _ _ R _ _ _   _ _   _ R _ _   _ _ _ _   _ _ _ _ _ _ _ :
LB  ZBHRCBABNL  QB  TAGQ  QRWB  BWBQRBV:

_ _ A ,   _ _ _ _   _ _ _ _ _ _ _   _ _   _ _   A _ _ _ _   _ _ _ _ _
XBU,  NLGF  HRTNBVN  QB  FE  UPGCB  NLGVB

_ _ A _   R _ _ _   _ _   A _ A _ _ _ _   _ _ :   _ _ _ _   _ A _ _
NLUN  ARVB  FE  UKURWVN  QB:  NLGF  LUVN

_ _ _ _ _ _ R _ _   _ _   _ R _ _   _ _ _   _ _ _ _ _ _ _   _ A _ .
ZBHRCBABZ  QB  TAGQ  NLB  CRGHBWN  QUW.
```

264

```
___  __  _____  ____  ____  ___  ___,
ETQ  SK  RKKDS  DSHD  MGRK  WKY  FGK,

                                B_U____
_____  ___  ____  ___  ___  
XGBKMGRK  DSK  ETTX  HYF  DSK  JQCDGRS

_____  _____,  ___  _____  _____
AKQRTY  AKQGRS,  HYF  XKHUK  DSKGQ

_____  __  _____.
MKHXDS  DT  TDSKQR.
```

- -

265

```
___  __  ___  ____  __  _____  __  _____
XFD  LE  ZOU  ZLBU  FX  ZDFTVKU  OU  YOQKK

                                     C
____  __  __  ___  _____:  __  ___  __C____
OLHU  BU  LE  OLY  RQSLKLFE:  LE  ZOU  YUJDUZ

            C
__  ___  _____C__  _____  __  ____  __;
FX  OLY  ZQVUDEQJKU  YOQKK  OU  OLHU  BU;

                             __CK.
__  _____  ___  __  __  ____  _  __CK.
OU  YOQKK  YUZ  BU  TR  TRFE  Q  DFJM.
```

- -

266

```
                D
_____  __  __  ____D____  __  __  _____
AQCHC  ME  XG  EGTXRXCEE  MX  FW  BYCEQ

__C____  __  _____  _____;  _____  __
DCNVTEC  GB  AQMXC  VXKCH;  XCMAQCH  ME

                                 __C____
_____  ___  ____  __  __  _____  __C____
AQCHC  VXW  HCEA  MX  FW  DGXCE  DCNVTEC

__  __  ___.
GB  FW  EMX.
```

267

___ ___K__ ____ _____ ___ ___ _____,
BKS RJIXST KCLS TYCRM EVB BKS UREYT,

___ ____ ____ _____ ___, __ ____ ____
CMT KCLS NSMB BKSJY NER, BE ICUB TERM

___ ____ ___ _____, ___ __ ____ ____
BKS FEEY CMT MSSTZ, CMT BE UWCZ UVIK

__ __ __ ____G__ _____.
CU NS EA VFYJHKB IEMLSYUCBJEM.

268

__ __A_ __A__I____ ___ __A____, __A__
PC UPYU BPYRUHRCUP UPC PCYUPCD, RPYSS

___ __ _____? __ __A_ __A_____ _A_
DVU PC BVGGCBU? PC UPYU UCYBPCUP EYD

_____, __A__ ___ __ ____?
ADVOSCLZC, RPYSS DVU PC ADVO?

269

___ ____ ____ _____ __ ____ ____
SUK AEUJ ELRA BDVPMDKDB GQ RUJV SKUG

_____: ____ N__ ____ _____ __ ____
BDLAE: XPVA HUA AEUJ BDVPMDK GQ SDDA

____ _____N_, ____ _ ___ ____ _____
SKUG SLVVPHY, AELA P GLQ XLVC FDSUKD

G__ _N ___ _____ __ ___ ____N_?
YUB PH AED VPYEA US AED VPMPHY?

270

```
___   ___   _I____   ___S____   __   _IS
PNL   RAT   EXUVTB   DNCKRTRA   NP   AXK

_____'S   __SI__,   ___   ___SS___   ___
ATCLR'K     BTKXLT,   COB   DYTKKTRA   RAT

_____S,   ____   ___   ____   _____.
UNFTRNGK,    EANQ   RAT   YNLB   CDANLLTRA.
```

271

```
__E_   ____   ____   _EE_   ___E_   __   ___E
RKCP   MXTF   RKMR   TCCJ   MWRCV   YP   XEWC

___   ____E_   ___   _E:   ___   __E_   ____
XMP   TAMVCT   WFV   YC:   MAB   RKCP   RKMR

_EE_   __   ____   _PE__   _____E____   _____,
TCCJ   YP   KQVR   TDCMJ   YETGKECIFQT   RKEANT,

___   _____E   _E_E___   ___   __E   ___
MAB   EYMNEAC   BCGCERT   MXX   RKC   BMP

____.
XFAN.
```

272

```
____   __   ____   T__   _____T   _____   __
MYIT   DT   HUND   EMT   KTRUTE   RNAVKTF   NH

T__   _____;   ____   T__   _____T___   __
EMT   JYROTI;   HUND   EMT   YVKAUUTREYNV   NH

T__   _____   __   ___Q__T_:
EMT   JNUOTUK   NH   YVYZAYEQ:
```

273

_ _ _ _ _ _ , _ _ _ _ _ _ _ _ _ _ _ _ _ , _ _ _ _ _ _ _
CWBTKO, BW RETIW IBW DTNA, IBMI IBW

_ _ _ _ _ _ _ _ _ _ _ _ _ _ _ , _ _ _ _ _ _ _ _ _ _ _ _ _
SMIWDR VFRBWO TFI, MPO IBW RIDWMER

_ _ _ _ _ _ _ _ _ ; _ _ _ _ _ _ I _ _ _ _ _ _ _
TGWDXKTSWO; NMP BW VHGW CDWMO

_ _ _ _ ? _ _ _ _ _ P _ _ _ I _ _ _ _ _ _ _ _ _ _ _ I _
MKRT? NMP BW JDTGHOW XKWRB XTD BHR

P _ _ P _ _ ?
JWTJKW?

- -

274

_ O _ _ , _ _ _ _ _ _ _ _ _ _ T _ _ _ _ _ _ T _ T _ _ _ _ _
VHTX, F NBYM VHYMX ZNM NBQFZBZFHD HE

T _ _ _ _ _ _ _ , _ _ _ T _ _ _ _ _ _ _ _ _ _ _ _
ZNG NHOUM, BDX ZNM SVBAM CNMTM

T _ _ _ _ _ _ _ _ _ _ _ _ _ _ _ _ T _ .
ZNFDM NHDHOT XCMVVMZN.

- -

275

_ _ _ _ _ _ _ _ _ _ _ _ _ _ _ _ _ _ _ _ _ _ _ _ _ _ _ D _ _ _ _ ,
YAKZ RAI FGDLKWWMEY WMLSJOCSJXJKYY,

_ _ _ _ _ _ _ _ _ _ _ _ _ _ _ B _ _ _ _ _ _ _ _ _ _ _ _ D
M RAME RAGR YGLKYR PI RAI DSOAR AGJX

_ _ _ _ _ _ _ _ _ _ _ _ _ _ _ _ _ _ _ _ _ _ _ _ _ _ _ _
RAKF ZASQA TER RAKSD RDEYR SJ RAKK

_ _ _ _ _ _ _ _ _ _ _ _ _ _ _ _ _ _ _ _ _ _ _ _ _ _ _ _ _ _ .
UDMF RAMYK RAGR DSYK ET GOGSJYR RAKF.

276

```
_ _ _ _ _,  _  _ O _,  _ _ _ _ _   T _ _ _ _   O _ _   _ _ _ _ _ _:
XWCEN,    Z  RZP,  HONXP    KACTN    ZFT    YXBEN:

_ _ _ _ _ _ _ _   _ O _   T _ _   _ O O _ _ _ _   _ _ _
WNLNLDNW    AZF    KAN    IZZOCEA    LXT

_ _ _ _ O _ _ _ _ T _   T _ _ _   _ _ _ _ _.
WNHWZXYANKA    KANN    PXCOM.
```

277

```
_ _   _ _   _ _ _ _ _ E _ _   _   _ _ _ _ E _   _ P _ _   _ _ E
AZ    RC    PALHFWLL    A    BTKKWP    DMXZ    HSW

_ _ _ _,   _ _ _   _ _ _ E _   _ _ _ _   _ _   _ _ _:   _ E   _ E _ _ _
KXFP,    TZP    BFAWP    DZHX    RC    QXP:    SW    SWTFP

_ _   _ _ _ _ E   _ _ _   _ _   _ _ _   _ E _ P _ E,   _ _ _   _ _
RC    IXABW    XDH    XJ    SAL    HWRMKW,    TZP    RC

_ _ _   _ _ _ E   BE _ _ _ E   _ _ _,   E _ E _   _ _ _ _   _ _ _
BFC    BTRW    OWJXFW    SAR,    WIWZ    AZHX    SAL

E _ _ _.
WTFL.
```

278

```
_ _ _   _ O _   _ _ _   _ O O _   O _   _ _ _ _ _   _ O _ _
EHI    ZBI    ICH    RBBI    BR    JSQXH    LBUH

_ _ _ _ _ _ _   _ _,   _ _ _   _ _ _   _ O _   _ _ _   _ _ _ _   O _
MFMQZOI    UH,    MZX    EHI    ZBI    ICH    CMZX    BR

_ _ _   _ _ _ _ _ _   _ _ _ O V _   _ _.
ICH    PQLTHX    SHUBDH    UH.
```

279

_ _ _ I _ _ _ _ _ _ _, _ _ _ _ _ _ _ _, _ _ _ _ _
XWXYLUK KVCC, KVCC MLZI, VXJC Y

_ I _ _ _ _, _ _ _ _ _ _ _ _ _ I _ _ _ I _ I _ _ _ _
UYLLCQ, XLQ QMLC KVYU CJYZ YL KVI

_ I _ _ _: _ _ _ _ _ _ _ _ _ I _ _ _ _ _ _ _ _
UYWVK: KVXK KVMB EYWVKCUK DC

_ _ _ _ I F I _ _ _ _ _ _ _ _ _ _ _ _ _ _ K _ _ _, _ _ _ _ _
ABUKYPYCQ SVCL KVMB UFCXOCUK, XLQ DC

_ _ _ _ _ _ _ _ _ _ _ _ _ _ _ _ _ _ _ _.
HZCXN SVCL KVMB ABQWCUK.

- -

280

_ _ _ _ _ _ H _ _ _ _ _ H _ H _ _ _ _ _ _ _ _ _ _ _
EIMZON CZU VZAC ACN AZUFINW MTP

_ _ _ _ _: _ _ _ _ _ _ H _ _ _ _ _ H _ _ _ _ _ _ _ _
PMTHN: EIMZON CZU VZAC OAIZTRNP

_ _ _ _ _ U _ _ _ _ _ _ _ _ _ _ _ _ _ _.
ZTOAIGUNTAO MTP DIRMTO.

- -

281

_ _ _ _ _, _ _ I _ _ _ _ _ _ _ _ _ M _ _ _ _ I _ _,
QMB AW, QWXTF DMPP VD NVJSYRRXVT,

_ _ _ _ _ _ _ _ _ _ I _ I _ I _ _ I _ _, _ _ _
DVKFYUW BAWXK XTXHMXBI, YTC

_ _ _ _ _ _ _ _ _ _ _ _ _ M _ _ _: _ _ _, M _ _ _ _ _ I M _
CWRBKVIWC BAWJ TVB: IWY, JYTI Y BXJW

_ _ _ _ _ _ _ _ _ _ I _ _ _ _ _ _ _ _ _ _, _ _ _ _ I _ _ _ _
BMKTWC AW AXR YTFWK YZYI, YTC CXC TVB

_ _ I _ _ _ _ _ _ _ I _ _ _ _ _ _.
RBXK MS YPP AXR ZKYBA.

```
___ _____ ____ ____ __ ____, __
JRS SXLYO SXGS YOOV WZ YLRD, SL

D_____ __, _____ __ ____ ___ _____
MOYSTLZ KS, YXGDD FL KISL SXO DLAOT

_____ _F ___ _____.
NGTSY LC SXO OGTSX.
```

- -

```
___ ____ ___N _ __ __D _ND
KNJ EHLN JRAK G EB NHM EKM

___Y___D_D, _ __D, _____ __ N__;
UWEZRAEMAM, N UNM, TNWLESA BA KNY;

_N___ _ ____ _____D __Y ___ _N___
CKYGH G REIA LRAJAM YRZ LYWAKUYR

_N__ ____ __N_____N, _ND __Y _____
CKYN YRGL UAKAWEYGNK, EKM YRZ DNJAW

__ ____ _Y _N_ ____ __ __ ____.
YN AIAWZ NKA YREY GL YN ONBA.
```

- -

```
_O_ __O_O__O_ _O____ _____ F_O_
JCB FBCQCXLCM TCQKXI MKLXIKB JBCQ

___ ____, _O_ F_O_ ___ ____, _O_ F_O_
XIK KZPX, MCB JBCQ XIK NKPX, MCB JBCQ

___ _O___.
XIK PCEXI.
```

285

```
___ _____ ___ __ __ _____ F_____, _
JAG IMKQR AVR DP JX RQPMS OJRQPSX, J

_____ ___ _____ _____; _
XRNDDVSA JAG SPDPYYMVNX KPAPSJRMVA; J

_____ ____ ___ ___ _____ _____
KPAPSJRMVA RQJR XPR AVR RQPMS QPJSR

_____, ___ _____ _P____ ___ ___
JSMKQR, JAG CQVXP XWMSMR CJX AVR

____F___ ____ ___.
XRPGOJXR CMRQ KVG.
```

286

```
_E_ __E ____ _____E_ __ ___ _E _N
NJU UDJ DEYD TWVEFJF LR YLZ OJ ES

__E__ _____, _N_ _ ___E__E_ _____ _N
UDJEW QLAUD, VSZ V UHLJZYJZ FHLWZ ES

__E__ __N_;
UDJEW DVSZ;
```

287

```
____ __C_ ___ S_____ __S_ ____
ESSC RVJE PTO LSGXVHP VMLU DGUZ

___S_____S S__S; ___ ____ ___ ____
CGSLAZCPAUAL LNHL; MSP PTSZ HUP TVXS

_____ ____ __: ____ S____ _ __
WUZNHNUH UXSG ZS: PTSH LTVMM N RS

_____, ___ _ S____ __ ____C___
ACGNYTP, VHW N LTVMM RS NHHUJSHP

____ ___ _____ ____S___SS___.
DGUZ PTS YGSVP PGVHLYGSLLNUH.
```

288

```
___  ___G'_  ___G_T__  __  ___     G_____
CKI  NHGU'A  TRYUKCIS  HA  RMM  UMLSHLYA

__T___:  ___  ___T___G  __  __  ____G_T
ZHCKHG:  KIS  VMLCKHGU  HA  LE  ZSLYUKC

G_ _ _.
ULMT.
```

289

```
__  ___  ____  A__A__  ____  ___  __  _A__
KY  VNS  SFND  MGLMWB  QFYV  NVY  WI  HMBY

____,  ____  ___  G____  __  ___  _____  __
LWEF,  QFYV  SFY  ACNLT  NG  FWI  FNDIY  WI

_ _____A___;  ___  ____  __  _____  __  __A__
WVELYMIYB;  GNL  QFYV  FY  BWYSF  FY  IFMCC

_A___  _____ _G  A_A_:  ___  G____  __A__
EMLLT  VNSFWVA  MQMT:  FWI  ACNLT  IFMCC

___  _____  A____  ___ _.
VNS  BYIEYVB  MGSYL  FWH.
```

290

```
____  ___L_  _____  __  ____  ___
MXTY  PXEJM  RYUZB  DB  GUMX  MXO

C__ _ __L,  ___  _____  __C____  __  __
STYWPBJ,  EWZ  EAMBNGENZ  NBSBUCB  DB  MT

_L_ _.
RJTNO.
```

291

I _____ __ ___ ____ ____, ___
Q IBJYKEAHWNHW LM FQY PYVK VUHH, IYW

____ _____ ____ I ___ ___. I
LQYH QYQDPQVM UIOH Q YKV UQW. Q

___ _, I ____ ___F___ __
FIQW, Q EQAA BKYZHFF LM

_____ ____ ___ L__ _; ___
VCIYFNCHFFQKYF PYVK VUH AKCW; IYW

____ F_____ ___ _____ _F __
VUKP ZKCNIOHFV VUH QYQDPQVM KZ LM

___. _____.
FQY. FHAIU.

- -

292

__R ____, _ ___, ____ _R____ __: ____
TQL OMQN, Q PQR, MXDO ALQYZR ND: OMQN

____ _RI__ __, __ _I___R I_ _RI__.
MXDO OLVZR ND, XD DVJYZL VD OLVZR.

- -

293

T____ T_____ ___T T___ ____, ___ _
WDTET WDKURE DGEW WDYA CYUT, GUC K

___T _____; T___ T_____T__T T__T
ITHW EKQTUOT; WDYA WDYARDWTEW WDGW

_ ___ __T___T__ ____ __ ___ __
K SGE GQWYRTWDTZ EAOD GU YUT GE

T_____: __T _ ____ _____ T___, ___
WDFETQP: LAW K SKQQ ZTHZYXT WDTT, GUC

__T T___ __ ____ _____ T____ ____.
ETW WDTB KU YZCTZ LTPYZT WDKUT TFTE.

294

```
_ _ _ _    _ _    _ _ T _ _ _    _ _ _    _ _    _ _ T _ _ _
NUSX  QK   PIZUSW   IXH   QK   QVZUSW
```

```
_ _ _ _ _ _ _    _ _,    T _ _ _    T _ _    _ _ _ D    _ _ _ _    T _ _ _
PVWMIAS  QS,  ZUSX  ZUS  DVWH  NFDD  ZIAS
```

```
_ _    _ _.
QS  CO.
```

- -

295

```
_ _ _    _ _    _ _ _ _    _ _ _ _ _ _ _ _ _    _ H _ _    _ _ _ _ _ _ _ _,
FTZ  AW  IAWH  KSUHCBAZE  ZMHE  CHLYANHS,
```

```
_ _ _    _ _ _ H _ _ _ _    _ H _ _ _ L _ _    _ _ _ _ _ H _ _:
KWS  XKZMHCHS  ZMHIBHPUHB  ZYXHZMHC:
```

```
_ _ _,    _ H _    _ _ _ _ _ _ _    _ _ _ H _ _ _ _    _ H _ _ _ L _ _ _
EHK,  ZMH  KFLHNZB  XKZMHCHS  ZMHIBHPUHB
```

```
_ _ _ _ _ H _ _    _ _ _ _ _ _ _    _ _,    _ _ _    _ _ _ _    _ _
ZYXHZMHC  KXKAWBZ  IH,  KWS  A  GWHD  AZ
```

```
_ _ _;    _ H _ _    _ _ _    _ _ _ _    _ _,    _ _ _    _ _ _ _ _ _ _
WYZ;  ZMHE  SAS  ZHKC  IH,  KWS  NHKBHS
```

```
_ _ _:
WYZ:
```

- -

296

```
O    _ _ V _    _ _ _ _ _ _    _ _ _ _    _ _ _    _ _ _    _ _    _ _ _ V _ _:
D  QCKI  URGYBP  AYUD  URI  QDE  DW  RIGKIY:
```

```
_ _ _    _ _ _    _ _ _ _ _    _ _ _ _ _ _ _    _ _ _    _ V _ _.
WDL  RCP  FILXS  IYEALIUR  WDL  IKIL.
```

297

```
_ _A__ __T ___ T__ ____T_____
D YIRJ MGB YDP BYN UDWYBJGSQMJQQ

__T___ __ __A_T; _ _A__ ____A___ T__
ODBYDM HN YJIUB; D YIRJ PJLXIUJP BYN

_A_T_____ A__ T__ _A__AT___: _
KIDBYKSXMJQQ IMP BYN QIXRIBDGM: D

_A__ __T _____A___ T__
YIRJ MGB LGMLJIXJP BYN

_____ A__ T__ T__T_ ____
XGRDMWCDMPMJQQ IMP BYN BUSBY KUGH

T__ ___AT _____AT___.
BYJ WUJIB LGMWUJWIBDGM.
```

- -

298

```
__ ____, ____ ____ ____ _P__ ___; ___
AE PUXC, MYFQ QZUX ULCE XRUL SUT; DUG

__ E_PE_____ __ ____ ___.
AE JBRJKQYQFUL FP DGUA ZFA.
```

- -

299

```
_ Y_ ____ __ ___, __W ____ W___ Y_
M CB KMRK MZ FBR, JMA QMRP ASQQ CB

____ _Y ____Y ____ _____? __W ____
HTIR FC PQMIC SRHM KJDFB? JMA QMRP

W___ Y_ ____ _____Y, ___ ____ _____
ASQQ CB QMGB GDRSHC, DRO KBBY DZHBI

_____? _____.
QBDKSRP? KBQDJ.
```

300

```
___   ____   __   ___   _____   ___
AGX   EWON   BZ   BPK   OXWKN   WKX

T_____   _____   _N_ T_N;   _N_   __   __
AGKXXNTBKX   OXWKN   WDE   AXD;   WDE   QZ   HO

_____N   __   _T__N_T_   T___   __
KXWNBD   BZ   NAKXDMAG   AGXO   HX

_____   _____, __T __ T____
ZBPKNTBKX   OXWKN,   OXA   QN   AGXQK

_T__N_T_   _____   _N_   _____;   ___   _T
NAKXDMAG   FWHBPK   WDE   NBKKBR;   ZBK   QA

__   ___N __T ___, _N_ __ ___ ____.
QN   NBBD   TPA   BZZ,   WDE   RX   ZFO   WRWO.
```

301

```
_R___ __ S___ _____ ____ ___: _R__
EOLRH   BH   YILR   DUXESEJ   LQIM   CIW:   KOIB

___ _____ __ S_____.
JXB   NIBSEJ   BH   YURAUEXIM.
```

302

```
___ _____ __ ___ ____ _____ __V_
ZMR   MPZRAE   KJ   ZMR   GKAX   EMKVGX   MPDR

__B_____ _____V__ ____ ___: B__
EVIOUZZRX   ZMROERGDRE   VBZK   MUO:   IVZ

_____ ____ _____ __V_ _____ ___
ZMRUA   ZUOR   EMKVGX   MPDR   RBXVARX   JKA

_V__.
RDRA.
```

303

```
_E____ ____ _E, _LL _E ____E__ __
VOGSEI XEJN NO, SKK QO BJEDOEM JX

I_I__I__; ___ __E ____ ____ _E___ __E
ZCZRTZIQ; XJE IYO KJEV YSIY YOSEV IYO

__I_E __ __ _EE_I__.
AJZUO JX NQ BOOGZCF.
```

- -

304

```
H___, _O__; ___ ___ _____ ___ _____ _;
WIRF, RUEH; LUE SWI VUHRJ ZBA XIBGISW;

___ ___ _____ ____ ____ _____ ___
LUE SWI LBNSWLPR LBNR LEUZ BZUAV SWI

_ _____ __ ___.
XWNRHEIA UL ZIA.
```

- -

305

```
___ _H_ ____ __U____H __ _H_ ___D,
AHP MJR QSWE MPCUMRMJ SW MJR ZHPN,

___ _H__U_H _H_ _____ __ _H_ ____ _
VWN MJPHCEJ MJR ORPDI HA MJR OHUM

___H H_ _H___ ___ __ _____.
JSEJ JR UJVZZ WHM FR OHXRN.
```

- -

306

```
_____ __, _ __R_; ___ _ ____ ___K__ __
ALPNB RB, F SFCP; ZFC D OWEB IWSGBP DX

____ _____Y: _ ____ _____ ____
RDXB DXQBNCDQJ: D OWEB QCLYQBP WSYF

__ ___ __R_; _____ _ ____ ___
DX QOB SFCP; QOBCBZFCB D YOWSS XFQ

_____.
YSDPB.
```

Solutions

1. Give us help from trouble: for vain is the help of man. 108:12
2. Thou hast commanded us to keep thy precepts diligently. 119:4
3. Wherefore should the heathen say, Where is now their God? 115:2
4. The LORD knoweth the thoughts of man, that they are vanity. 94:11
5. The LORD that made heaven and earth bless thee out of Zion. 134:3
6. O LORD our Lord, how excellent is thy name in all the earth! 8:9
7. God is our refuge and strength, a very present help in trouble. 46:1
8. My meditation of him shall be sweet: I will be glad in the LORD. 104:34
9. Arise, O LORD, into thy rest; thou, and the ark of thy strength. 132:8
10. It is better to trust in the LORD than to put confidence in man. 118:8
11. What shall I render unto the LORD for all his benefits toward me? 116:12
12. The LORD is on my side; I will not fear: what can man do unto me? 118:6
13. If thou, LORD, shouldest mark iniquities, O Lord, who shall stand? 130:3
14. Man goeth forth unto his work and to his labour until the evening. 104:23
15. The LORD is righteous: he hath cut asunder the cords of the wicked. 129:4
16. My knees are weak through fasting; and my flesh faileth of fatness. 109:24
17. Pray for the peace of Jerusalem: they shall prosper that love thee. 122:6
18. The LORD preserveth the simple: I was brought low, and he helped me. 116:6
19. The dead praise not the LORD, neither any that go down into silence. 115:17
20. I will sing unto the LORD, because he hath dealt bountifully with me. 13:6
21. Defend the poor and fatherless: do justice to the afflicted and needy. 82:3

Solutions

22. Remove from me reproach and contempt; for I have kept thy testimonies. 119:22
23. Create in me a clean heart, O God; and renew a right spirit within me. 51:10
24. The idols of the heathen are silver and gold, the work of men's hands. 135:15
25. Deliver my soul, O LORD, from lying lips, and from a deceitful tongue. 120:2
26. O God, thou knowest my foolishness; and my sins are not hid from thee. 69:5
27. But our God is in the heavens: he hath done whatsoever he hath pleased. 115:3
28. The LORD lifteth up the meek: he casteth the wicked down to the ground. 147:6
29. Turn us again, O God, and cause thy face to shine; and we shall be saved. 80:3
30. For all the gods of the nations are idols: but the LORD made the heavens. 96:5
31. For my soul is full of troubles: and my life draweth nigh unto the grave. 88:3
32. The LORD executeth righteousness and judgment for all that are oppressed. 103:6
33. So teach us to number our days, that we may apply our hearts unto wisdom. 90:12
34. The Lord gave the word: great was the company of those that published it. 68:11
35. The LORD hath chastened me sore: but he hath not given me over unto death. 118:18
36. The wicked shall be turned into hell, and all the nations that forget God. 9:17
37. Keep not thou silence, O God: hold not thy peace, and be not still, O God. 83:1
38. How sweet are thy words unto my taste! yea, sweeter than honey to my mouth! 119:103
39. Their land brought forth frogs in abundance, in the chambers of their kings. 105:30
40. O come, let us worship and bow down: let us kneel before the LORD our maker. 95:6
41. Blessed be God, which hath not turned away my prayer, nor his mercy from me. 66:20
42. The high hills are a refuge for the wild goats; and the rocks for the conies. 104:18

Solutions

43. Cease from anger, and forsake wrath: fret not thyself in any wise to do evil. 37:8
44. O LORD, rebuke me not in thy wrath: neither chasten me in thy hot displeasure. 38:1
45. Save now, I beseech thee, O LORD: O LORD, I beseech thee, send now prosperity. 118:25
46. The works of his hands are verity and judgment; all his commandments are sure. 111:7
47. Like as a father pitieth his children, so the LORD pitieth them that fear him. 103:13
48. Commit thy way unto the LORD; trust also in him; and he shall bring it to pass. 37:5
49. The LORD also will be a refuge for the oppressed, a refuge in times of trouble. 9:9
50. O taste and see that the LORD is good: blessed is the man that trusteth in him. 34:8
51. Behold, how good and how pleasant it is for brethren to dwell together in unity! 133:1
52. The LORD is gracious, and full of compassion; slow to anger, and of great mercy. 145:8
53. The fire consumed their young men; and their maidens were not given to marriage. 78:63
54. How precious also are thy thoughts unto me, O God! how great is the sum of them! 139:17
55. Be thou exalted, O God, above the heavens; let thy glory be above all the earth. 57:5
56. Great is the LORD, and greatly to be praised; and his greatness is unsearchable. 145:3
57. O LORD, rebuke me not in thine anger, neither chasten me in thy hot displeasure. 6:1
58. I will remember the works of the LORD: surely I will remember thy wonders of old. 77:11
59. They reel to and fro, and stagger like a drunken man, and are at their wits' end. 107:27
60. As the hart panteth after the water brooks, so panteth my soul after thee, O God. 42:1
61. He that sitteth in the heavens shall laugh: the Lord shall have them in derision. 2:4
62. God be merciful unto us, and bless us; and cause his face to shine upon us; Selah. 67:1
63. I will praise the name of God with a song, and will magnify him with thanksgiving. 69:30

Solutions

64. Bow thy heavens, O LORD, and come down: touch the mountains, and they shall smoke. 144:5
65. He turneth the wilderness into a standing water, and dry ground into watersprings. 107:35
66. Lo, children are an heritage of the LORD: and the fruit of the womb is his reward. 127:3
67. Through God we shall do valiantly: for he it is that shall tread down our enemies. 60:12
68. We have sinned with our fathers, we have committed iniquity, we have done wickedly. 106:6
69. But thou, O LORD, shalt laugh at them; thou shalt have all the heathen in derision. 59:8
70. For the LORD will not cast off his people, neither will he forsake his inheritance. 94:14
71. Exalt the LORD our God, and worship at his holy hill; for the LORD our God is holy. 99:9
72. Be thou exalted, LORD, in thine own strength: so will we sing and praise thy power. 21:13
73. Delight thyself also in the LORD; and he shall give thee the desires of thine heart. 37:4
74. The angel of the LORD encampeth round about them that fear him, and delivereth them. 34:7
75. The LORD liveth; and blessed be my rock; and let the God of my salvation be exalted. 18:46
76. Concerning thy testimonies, I have known of old that thou hast founded them for ever. 119:152
77. Make me to understand the way of thy precepts: so shall I talk of thy wondrous works. 119:27
78. For the righteous LORD loveth righteousness; his countenance doth behold the upright. 11:7
79. For the LORD taketh pleasure in his people: he will beautify the meek with salvation. 149:4
80. Princes have persecuted me without a cause: but my heart standeth in awe of thy word. 119:161
81. I will say of the LORD, He is my refuge and my fortress: my God; in him will I trust. 91:2
82. I will praise thee, O Lord, among the people: I will sing unto thee among the nations. 57:9
83. Come and see the works of God: he is terrible in his doing toward the children of men. 66:5
84. Come and hear, all ye that fear God, and I will declare what he hath done for my soul. 66:16

Solutions

85. He hath not dealt with us after our sins; nor rewarded us according to our iniquities. 103:10
86. Do good, O LORD, unto those that be good, and to them that are upright in their hearts. 125:4
87. Those that be planted in the house of the LORD shall flourish in the courts of our God. 92:13
88. For the LORD knoweth the way of the righteous: but the way of the ungodly shall perish. 1:6
89. For thou hast maintained my right and my cause; thou satest in the throne judging right. 9:4
90. What man is he that feareth the LORD? him shall he teach in the way that he shall choose. 25:12
91. For the LORD is good; his mercy is everlasting; and his truth endureth to all generations. 100:5
92. Give unto the LORD the glory due unto his name; worship the LORD in the beauty of holiness. 29:2
93. I have set the LORD always before me: because he is at my right hand, I shall not be moved. 16:8
94. Thou, even thou, art to be feared: and who may stand in thy sight when once thou art angry? 76:7
95. From the rising of the sun unto the going down of the same the LORD'S name is to be praised. 113:3
96. Wherewithal shall a young man cleanse his way? by taking heed thereto according to thy word. 119:9
97. He delighteth not in the strength of the horse: he taketh not pleasure in the legs of a man. 147:10
98. Praise the LORD with harp: sing unto him with the psaltery and an instrument of ten strings. 33:2
99. My flesh and my heart faileth: but God is the strength of my heart, and my portion for ever. 73:26
100. Thou shalt destroy them that speak leasing: the LORD will abhor the bloody and deceitful man. 5:6
101. LORD, thou hast been favourable unto thy land: thou hast brought back the captivity of Jacob. 85:1
102. Of old hast thou laid the foundation of the earth: and the heavens are the work of thy hands. 102:25
103. I know, O LORD, that thy judgments are right, and that thou in faithfulness hast afflicted me. 119:75
104. Some trust in chariots, and some in horses: but we will remember the name of the LORD our God. 20:7
105. The wicked are estranged from the womb: they go astray as soon as they be born, speaking lies. 58:3

Solutions

106. That men may know that thou, whose name alone is JEHOVAH, art the most high over all the earth. 83:18
107. Ascribe ye strength unto God: his excellency is over Israel, and his strength is in the clouds. 68:34
108. Fret not thyself because of evildoers, neither be thou envious against the workers of iniquity. 37:1
109. Though the LORD be high, yet hath he respect unto the lowly: but the proud he knoweth afar off. 138:6
110. When their judges are overthrown in stony places, they shall hear my words; for they are sweet. 141:6
111. I had fainted, unless I had believed to see the goodness of the LORD in the land of the living. 27:13
112. He hath remembered his covenant for ever, the word which he commanded to a thousand generations. 105:8
113. Thy word is true from the beginning: and every one of thy righteous judgments endureth for ever. 119:160
114. Let us come before his presence with thanksgiving, and make a joyful noise unto him with psalms. 95:2
115. All the paths of the LORD are mercy and truth unto such as keep his covenant and his testimonies. 25:10
116. I will not be afraid of ten thousands of people, that have set themselves against me round about. 3:6
117. We are become a reproach to our neighbours, a scorn and derision to them that are round about us. 79:4
118. The words of the LORD are pure words: as silver tried in a furnace of earth, purified seven times. 12:6
119. Therefore I esteem all thy precepts concerning all things to be right; and I hate every false way. 119:128
120. The LORD on high is mightier than the noise of many waters, yea, than the mighty waves of the sea. 93:4
121. For thou shalt eat the labour of thine hands: happy shalt thou be, and it shall be well with thee. 128:2
122. The LORD is nigh unto them that are of a broken heart; and saveth such as be of a contrite spirit. 34:18
123. That they might set their hope in God, and not forget the works of God, but keep his commandments: 78:7
124. Quicken me, O LORD, for thy name's sake: for thy righteousness' sake bring my soul out of trouble. 143:11
125. By the word of the LORD were the heavens made; and all the host of them by the breath of his mouth. 33:6
126. He that dwelleth in the secret place of the most High shall abide under the shadow of the Almighty. 91:1

Solutions

127. Let Israel hope in the LORD: for with the LORD there is mercy, and with him is plenteous redemption. 130:7
128. He maketh the barren woman to keep house, and to be a joyful mother of children. Praise ye the LORD. 113:9
129. For a thousand years in thy sight are but as yesterday when it is past, and as a watch in the night. 90:4
130. Wait on the LORD: be of good courage, and he shall strengthen thine heart: wait, I say, on the LORD. 27:14
131. Be glad in the LORD, and rejoice, ye righteous: and shout for joy, all ye that are upright in heart. 32:11
132. Clouds and darkness are round about him: righteousness and judgment are the habitation of his throne. 97:2
133. Many sorrows shall be to the wicked: but he that trusteth in the LORD, mercy shall compass him about. 32:10
134. In God I will praise his word, in God I have put my trust; I will not fear what flesh can do unto me. 56:4
135. Deliver me, O my God, out of the hand of the wicked, out of the hand of the unrighteous and cruel man. 71:4
136. Do not I hate them, O LORD, that hate thee? and am not I grieved with those that rise up against thee? 139:21
137. Be still, and know that I am God: I will be exalted among the heathen, I will be exalted in the earth. 46:10
138. My soul shall be satisfied as with marrow and fatness; and my mouth shall praise thee with joyful lips: 63:5
139. Our soul is escaped as a bird out of the snare of the fowlers: the snare is broken, and we are escaped. 124:7
140. O LORD, how manifold are thy works! in wisdom hast thou made them all: the earth is full of thy riches. 104:24
141. The sacrifices of God are a broken spirit: a broken and a contrite heart, O God, thou wilt not despise. 51:17
142. Blessed is the nation whose God is the LORD; and the people whom he hath chosen for his own inheritance. 33:12
143. Whoso is wise, and will observe these things, even they shall understand the lovingkindness of the LORD. 107:43
144. I will go in the strength of the Lord GOD: I will make mention of thy righteousness, even of thine only. 71:16
145. He brought them forth also with silver and gold: and there was not one feeble person among their tribes. 105:37
146. For thou, Lord, art good, and ready to forgive; and plenteous in mercy unto all them that call upon thee. 86:5
147. The wicked, through the pride of his countenance, will not seek after God: God is not in all his thoughts. 10:4

Solutions

148. I have been young, and now am old; yet have I not seen the righteous forsaken, nor his seed begging bread. 37:25
149. Behold, thou desirest truth in the inward parts: and in the hidden part thou shalt make me to know wisdom. 51:6
150. Confounded be all they that serve graven images, that boast themselves of idols: worship him, all ye gods. 97:7
151. Cast thy burden upon the LORD, and he shall sustain thee: he shall never suffer the righteous to be moved. 55:22
152. The LORD bringeth the counsel of the heathen to nought: he maketh the devices of the people of none effect. 33:10
153. Blessed is the people that know the joyful sound: they shall walk, O LORD, in the light of thy countenance. 89:15
154. There be many that say, Who will shew us any good? LORD, lift thou up the light of thy countenance upon us. 4:6
155. Unto the upright there ariseth light in the darkness: he is gracious, and full of compassion, and righteous. 112:4
156. Remember this, that the enemy hath reproached, O LORD, and that the foolish people have blasphemed thy name. 74:18
157. Attend unto my cry; for I am brought very low: deliver me from my persecutors; for they are stronger than I. 142:6
158. My hands also will I lift up unto thy commandments, which I have loved; and I will meditate in thy statutes. 119:48
159. For I have said, Mercy shall be built up for ever: thy faithfulness shalt thou establish in the very heavens. 89:2
160. I will praise the LORD according to his righteousness: and will sing praise to the name of the LORD most high. 7:17
161. But thou, O Lord, art a God full of compassion, and gracious, longsuffering, and plenteous in mercy and truth. 86:15
162. As for God, his way is perfect: the word of the LORD is tried: he is a buckler to all those that trust in him. 18:30
163. Judge me, O God, and plead my cause against an ungodly nation: O deliver me from the deceitful and unjust man. 43:1
164. Grant not, O LORD, the desires of the wicked: further not his wicked device; lest they exalt themselves. Selah. 140:8
165. Our soul is exceedingly filled with the scorning of those that are at ease, and with the contempt of the proud. 123:4
166. I will set no wicked thing before mine eyes: I hate the work of them that turn aside; it shall not cleave to me. 101:3
167. The LORD openeth the eyes of the blind: the LORD raiseth them that are bowed down: the LORD loveth the righteous: 146:8
168. The heavens are thine, the earth also is thine: as for the world and the fulness thereof, thou hast founded them. 89:11

Solutions

169. Ye that fear the LORD, praise him; all ye the seed of Jacob, glorify him; and fear him, all ye the seed of Israel. 22:23
170. The LORD rewarded me according to my righteousness; according to the cleanness of my hands hath he recompensed me. 18:20
171. Withhold not thou thy tender mercies from me, O LORD: let thy lovingkindness and thy truth continually preserve me. 40:11
172. O love the LORD, all ye his saints: for the LORD preserveth the faithful, and plentifully rewardeth the proud doer. 31:23
173. My soul longeth, yea, even fainteth for the courts of the LORD: my heart and my flesh crieth out for the living God. 84:2
174. My voice shalt thou hear in the morning, O LORD; in the morning will I direct my prayer unto thee, and will look up. 5:3
175. Vow, and pay unto the LORD your God: let all that be round about him bring presents unto him that ought to be feared. 76:11
176. God is greatly to be feared in the assembly of the saints, and to be had in reverence of all them that are about him. 89:7
177. Surely goodness and mercy shall follow me all the days of my life: and I will dwell in the house of the LORD for ever. 23:6
178. The LORD is in his holy temple, the LORD'S throne is in heaven: his eyes behold, his eyelids try, the children of men. 11:4
179. But I am poor and needy; yet the Lord thinketh upon me: thou art my help and my deliverer; make no tarrying, O my God. 40:17
180. In the day of my trouble I sought the Lord: my sore ran in the night, and ceased not: my soul refused to be comforted. 77:2
181. Unto thee, O God, do we give thanks, unto thee do we give thanks: for that thy name is near thy wondrous works declare. 75:1
182. Bless the LORD, ye his angels, that excel in strength, that do his commandments, hearkening unto the voice of his word. 103:20
183. I will sing a new song unto thee, O God: upon a psaltery and an instrument of ten strings will I sing praises unto thee. 144:9
184. From the end of the earth will I cry unto thee, when my heart is overwhelmed: lead me to the rock that is higher than I. 61:2

Solutions

185. How excellent is thy lovingkindness, O God! therefore the children of men put their trust under the shadow of thy wings. 36:7
186. They have said, Come, and let us cut them off from being a nation; that the name of Israel may be no more in remembrance. 83:4
187. Help us, O God of our salvation, for the glory of thy name: and deliver us, and purge away our sins, for thy name's sake. 79:9
188. For his anger endureth but a moment; in his favour is life: weeping may endure for a night, but joy cometh in the morning. 30:5
189. Thou wilt shew me the path of life: in thy presence is fulness of joy; at thy right hand there are pleasures for evermore. 16:11
190. The chariots of God are twenty thousand, even thousands of angels: the Lord is among them, as in Sinai, in the holy place. 68:17
191. Ye that love the LORD, hate evil: he preserveth the souls of his saints; he delivereth them out of the hand of the wicked. 97:10
192. I looked on my right hand, and beheld, but there was no man that would know me: refuge failed me; no man cared for my soul. 142:4
193. Remember, O LORD, the children of Edom in the day of Jerusalem; who said, Rase it, rase it, even to the foundation thereof. 137:7
194. I will praise thee; for I am fearfully and wonderfully made: marvellous are thy works; and that my soul knoweth right well. 139:14
195. The LORD preserveth the strangers; he relieveth the fatherless and widow: but the way of the wicked he turneth upside down. 146:9
196. He brought me up also out of an horrible pit, out of the miry clay, and set my feet upon a rock, and established my goings. 40:2
197. Let the words of my mouth, and the meditation of my heart, be acceptable in thy sight, O LORD, my strength, and my redeemer. 19:14
198. The wicked shall see it, and be grieved; he shall gnash with his teeth, and melt away: the desire of the wicked shall perish. 112:10
199. Oh let the wickedness of the wicked come to an end; but establish the just: for the righteous God trieth the hearts and reins. 7:9

Solutions

200. Now know I that the LORD saveth his anointed; he will hear him from his holy heaven with the saving strength of his right hand. 20:6
201. Let not them that are mine enemies wrongfully rejoice over me: neither let them wink with the eye that hate me without a cause. 35:19
202. God setteth the solitary in families: he bringeth out those which are bound with chains: but the rebellious dwell in a dry land. 68:6
203. Hide not thy face from me in the day when I am in trouble; incline thine ear unto me: in the day when I call answer me speedily. 102:2
204. Remember not the sins of my youth, nor my transgressions: according to thy mercy remember thou me for thy goodness' sake, O LORD. 25:7
205. Our God shall come, and shall not keep silence: a fire shall devour before him, and it shall be very tempestuous round about him. 50:3
206. Know ye that the LORD he is God: it is he that hath made us, and not we ourselves; we are his people, and the sheep of his pasture. 100:3
207. When the wicked spring as the grass, and when all the workers of iniquity do flourish; it is that they shall be destroyed for ever: 92:7
208. Let them be ashamed and confounded that seek after my soul: let them be turned backward, and put to confusion, that desire my hurt. 70:2
209. O sing unto the LORD a new song; for he hath done marvellous things: his right hand, and his holy arm, hath gotten him the victory. 98:1
210. Shew me a token for good; that they which hate me may see it, and be ashamed: because thou, LORD, hast holpen me, and comforted me. 86:17
211. Mine eyes shall be upon the faithful of the land, that they may dwell with me: he that walketh in a perfect way, he shall serve me. 101:6
212. He hath remembered his mercy and his truth toward the house of Israel: all the ends of the earth have seen the salvation of our God. 98:3
213. Say unto God, How terrible art thou in thy works! through the greatness of thy power shall thine enemies submit themselves unto thee. 66:3

Solutions

214. For the LORD loveth judgment, and forsaketh not his saints; they are preserved for ever: but the seed of the wicked shall be cut off. 37:28

215. Let them be confounded and put to shame that seek after my soul: let them be turned back and brought to confusion that devise my hurt. 35:4

216. Surely men of low degree are vanity, and men of high degree are a lie: to be laid in the balance, they are altogether lighter than vanity. 62:9

217. And he shall bring upon them their own iniquity, and shall cut them off in their own wickedness; yea, the LORD our God shall cut them off. 94:23

218. I will hear what God the LORD will speak: for he will speak peace unto his people, and to his saints: but let them not turn again to folly. 85:8

219. Thou hast turned for me my mourning into dancing: thou hast put off my sackcloth, and girded me with gladness; To the end that my glory may sing praise to thee, and not be silent. O LORD my God, I will give thanks unto thee for ever. 30:11-12

220. The fear of the LORD is the beginning of wisdom: a good understanding have all they that do his commandments: his praise endureth for ever. 111:10

221. Great is the LORD, and greatly to be praised in the city of our God, in the mountain of his holiness. Beautiful for situation, the joy of the whole earth, is mount Zion, on the sides of the north, the city of the great King. 48:1-2

222. He causeth the vapours to ascend from the ends of the earth; he maketh lightnings for the rain; he bringeth the wind out of his treasuries. 135:7

223. Many, O LORD my God, are thy wonderful works which thou hast done, and thy thoughts which are to us-ward: they cannot be reckoned up in order unto thee: if I would declare and speak of them, they are more than can be numbered. 40:5

224. Yea, they despised the pleasant land, they believed not his word:But murmured in their tents, and hearkened not unto the voice of the LORD. 106:24-25

225. But unto the wicked God saith, What hast thou to do to declare my statutes, or that thou shouldest take my covenant in thy mouth? Seeing thou hatest instruction, and castest my words behind thee. 50:16-17

Solutions

226. Yea, though I walk through the valley of the shadow of death, I will fear no evil: for thou art with me; thy rod and thy staff they comfort me. 23:4

227. One thing have I desired of the LORD, that will I seek after; that I may dwell in the house of the LORD all the days of my life, to behold the beauty of the LORD, and to enquire in his temple. 27:4

228. Before the mountains were brought forth, or ever thou hadst formed the earth and the world, even from everlasting to everlasting, thou art God. 90:2

229. What man is he that desireth life, and loveth many days, that he may see good? Keep thy tongue from evil, and thy lips from speaking guile. Depart from evil, and do good; seek peace, and pursue it. 34:12-14

230. Then was our mouth filled with laughter, and our tongue with singing: then said they among the heathen, The LORD hath done great things for them. 126:2

231. Blessed is the man whom thou choosest, and causest to approach unto thee, that he may dwell in thy courts: we shall be satisfied with the goodness of thy house, even of thy holy temple. 65:4

232. For a day in thy courts is better than a thousand. I had rather be a doorkeeper in the house of my God, than to dwell in the tents of wickedness. 84:10

233. Let them shout for joy, and be glad, that favour my righteous cause: yea, let them say continually, Let the LORD be magnified, which hath pleasure in the prosperity of his servant. 35:27

234. Why art thou cast down, O my soul? and why art thou disquieted in me? hope thou in God: for I shall yet praise him for the help of his countenance. 42:5

235. Thou visitest the earth, and waterest it: thou greatly enrichest it with the river of God, which is full of water: thou preparest them corn, when thou hast so provided for it. 65:9

236. Say among the heathen that the LORD reigneth: the world also shall be established that it shall not be moved: he shall judge the people righteously. 96:10

237. Be merciful unto me, O God, be merciful unto me: for my soul trusteth in thee: yea, in the shadow of thy wings will I make my refuge, until these calamities be overpast. 57:1

238. But I will sing of thy power; yea, I will sing aloud of thy mercy in the morning: for thou hast been my defence and refuge in the day of my trouble. 59:16

Solutions

239. Reproach hath broken my heart; and I am full of heaviness: and I looked for some to take pity, but there was none; and for comforters, but I found none. 69:20
240. For this shall every one that is godly pray unto thee in a time when thou mayest be found: surely in the floods of great waters they shall not come nigh unto him. 32:6
241. I will worship toward thy holy temple, and praise thy name for thy lovingkindness and for thy truth: for thou hast magnified thy word above all thy name. 138:2
242. Oh that the salvation of Israel were come out of Zion! When God bringeth back the captivity of his people, Jacob shall rejoice, and Israel shall be glad. 53:6
243. Oh how great is thy goodness, which thou hast laid up for them that fear thee; which thou hast wrought for them that trust in thee before the sons of men! 31:19
244. Then the channels of waters were seen, and the foundations of the world were discovered at thy rebuke, O LORD, at the blast of the breath of thy nostrils. 18:15
245. The LORD is my strength and my shield; my heart trusted in him, and I am helped: therefore my heart greatly rejoiceth; and with my song will I praise him. 28:7
246. For there they that carried us away captive required of us a song; and they that wasted us required of us mirth, saying, Sing us one of the songs of Zion. 137:3
247. Cause me to hear thy lovingkindness in the morning; for in thee do I trust: cause me to know the way wherein I should walk; for I lift up my soul unto thee. 143:8
248. Oh that the salvation of Israel were come out of Zion! when the LORD bringeth back the captivity of his people, Jacob shall rejoice, and Israel shall be glad. 14:7
249. Keep me as the apple of the eye, hide me under the shadow of thy wings, From the wicked that oppress me, from my deadly enemies, who compass me about. 17:8-9
250. The LORD is my rock, and my fortress, and my deliverer; my God, my strength, in whom I will trust; my buckler, and the horn of my salvation, and my high tower. 18:2
251. For they got not the land in possession by their own sword, neither did their own arm save them: but thy right hand, and thine arm, and the light of thy countenance, because thou hadst a favour unto them. 44:3
252. Keep me, O LORD, from the hands of the wicked; preserve me from the violent man; who have purposed to overthrow my goings. 140:4

Solutions

253. The LORD shall judge the people: judge me, O LORD, according to my righteousness, and according to mine integrity that is in me. 7:8
254. Wait on the LORD, and keep his way, and he shall exalt thee to inherit the land: when the wicked are cut off, thou shalt see it. 37:34
255. LORD, my heart is not haughty, nor mine eyes lofty: neither do I exercise myself in great matters, or in things too high for me. 131:1
256. But unto the wicked God saith, What hast thou to do to declare my statutes, or that thou shouldest take my covenant in thy mouth? 50:16
257. The fool hath said in his heart, There is no God. They are corrupt, they have done abominable works, there is none that doeth good. 14:1
258. But the king shall rejoice in God; every one that sweareth by him shall glory: but the mouth of them that speak lies shall be stopped. 63:11
259. The words of his mouth were smoother than butter, but war was in his heart: his words were softer than oil, yet were they drawn swords. 55:21
260. Why leap ye, ye high hills? this is the hill which God desireth to dwell in; yea, the LORD will dwell in it for ever. 68:16
261. When thou with rebukes dost correct man for iniquity, thou makest his beauty to consume away like a moth: surely every man is vanity. Selah. 39:11
262. According to thy name, O God, so is thy praise unto the ends of the earth: thy right hand is full of righteousness. 48:10
263. He delivereth me from mine enemies: yea, thou liftest me up above those that rise up against me: thou hast delivered me from the violent man. 18:48
264. For he seeth that wise men die, likewise the fool and the brutish person perish, and leave their wealth to others. 49:10
265. For in the time of trouble he shall hide me in his pavilion: in the secret of his tabernacle shall he hide me; he shall set me up upon a rock. 27:5
266. There is no soundness in my flesh because of thine anger; neither is there any rest in my bones because of my sin. 38:3
267. The wicked have drawn out the sword, and have bent their bow, to cast down the poor and needy, and to slay such as be of upright conversation. 37:14
268. He that chastiseth the heathen, shall not he correct? he that teacheth man knowledge, shall not he know? 94:10

Solutions

269. For thou hast delivered my soul from death: wilt not thou deliver my feet from falling, that I may walk before God in the light of the living? 56:13
270. For the wicked boasteth of his heart's desire, and blesseth the covetous, whom the LORD abhorreth. 10:3
271. They also that seek after my life lay snares for me: and they that seek my hurt speak mischievous things, and imagine deceits all the day long. 38:12
272. Hide me from the secret counsel of the wicked; from the insurrection of the workers of iniquity: 64:2
273. Behold, he smote the rock, that the waters gushed out, and the streams overflowed; can he give bread also? can he provide flesh for his people? 78:20
274. LORD, I have loved the habitation of thy house, and the place where thine honour dwelleth. 26:8
275. Shew thy marvellous lovingkindness, O thou that savest by thy right hand them which put their trust in thee from those that rise up against them. 17:7
276. Arise, O God, plead thine own cause: remember how the foolish man reproacheth thee daily. 74:22
277. In my distress I called upon the LORD, and cried unto my God: he heard my voice out of his temple, and my cry came before him, even into his ears. 18:6
278. Let not the foot of pride come against me, and let not the hand of the wicked remove me. 36:11
279. Against thee, thee only, have I sinned, and done this evil in thy sight: that thou mightest be justified when thou speakest, and be clear when thou judgest. 51:4
280. Praise him with the timbrel and dance: praise him with stringed instruments and organs. 150:4
281. But he, being full of compassion, forgave their iniquity, and destroyed them not: yea, many a time turned he his anger away, and did not stir up all his wrath. 78:38
282. But those that seek my soul, to destroy it, shall go into the lower parts of the earth. 63:9
283. Now also when I am old and grayheaded, O God, forsake me not; until I have shewed thy strength unto this generation, and thy power to every one that is to come. 71:18
284. For promotion cometh neither from the east, nor from the west, nor from the south. 75:6

Solutions

285. And might not be as their fathers, a stubborn and rebellious generation; a generation that set not their heart aright, and whose spirit was not stedfast with God. 78:8
286. Let the high praises of God be in their mouth, and a twoedged sword in their hand; 149:6
287. Keep back thy servant also from presumptuous sins; let them not have dominion over me: then shall I be upright, and I shall be innocent from the great transgression. 19:13
288. The king's daughter is all glorious within: her clothing is of wrought gold. 45:13
289. Be not thou afraid when one is made rich, when the glory of his house is increased; For when he dieth he shall carry nothing away: his glory shall not descend after him. 49:16-17
290. Thou shalt guide me with thy counsel, and afterward receive me to glory. 73:24
291. I acknowledged my sin unto thee, and mine iniquity have I not hid. I said, I will confess my transgressions unto the LORD; and thou forgavest the iniquity of my sin. Selah. 32:5
292. For thou, O God, hast proved us: thou hast tried us, as silver is tried. 66:10
293. These things hast thou done, and I kept silence; thou thoughtest that I was altogether such an one as thyself: but I will reprove thee, and set them in order before thine eyes. 50:21
294. When my father and my mother forsake me, then the LORD will take me up. 27:10
295. But in mine adversity they rejoiced, and gathered themselves together: yea, the abjects gathered themselves together against me, and I knew it not; they did tear me, and ceased not: 35:15
296. O give thanks unto the God of heaven: for his mercy endureth for ever. 136:26
297. I have not hid thy righteousness within my heart; I have declared thy faithfulness and thy salvation: I have not concealed thy lovingkindness and thy truth from the great congregation. 40:10
298. My soul, wait thou only upon God; for my expectation is from him. 62:5
299. O ye sons of men, how long will ye turn my glory into shame? how long will ye love vanity, and seek after leasing? Selah. 4:2

Solutions

300. The days of our years are threescore years and ten; and if by reason of strength they be fourscore years, yet is their strength labour and sorrow; for it is soon cut off, and we fly away. 90:10
301. Truly my soul waiteth upon God: from him cometh my salvation. 62:1
302. The haters of the LORD should have submitted themselves unto him: but their time should have endured for ever. 81:15
303. Depart from me, all ye workers of iniquity; for the LORD hath heard the voice of my weeping. 6:8
304. Help, LORD; for the godly man ceaseth; for the faithful fail from among the children of men. 12:1
305. For the king trusteth in the LORD, and through the mercy of the most High he shall not be moved. 21:7
306. Judge me, O LORD; for I have walked in mine integrity: I have trusted also in the LORD; therefore I shall not slide. 26:1

www.ingramcontent.com/pod-product-compliance
Lightning Source LLC
Chambersburg PA
CBHW081537120626
46550CB00009B/2760